Bauwelt Fundamente 155

Anja Schwanhäußer (ed)

Sensing the City

A Companion to Urban Anthropology

Bauverlag
Gütersloh · Berlin

Birkhäuser
Basel

The Bauwelt Fundamente series was founded in 1963 by Ulrich Conrads, who served as series editor until volume 149 in 2013, from the early 1980s jointly with Peter Neitzke.

Front and back cover: Nele Brönner

Library of Congress Cataloging-in-Publication data
A CIP catalog record for this book has been applied for at the Library of Congress.

Bibliographic information published by the German National Library
The German National Library lists this publication in the Deutsche Nationalbibliografie; detailed bibliographic data are available on the Internet at http://dnb.dnb.de.

This publication is also available as an e-book (ISBN PDF 978-3-0356-0735-2; ISBN EPUB 978-3-0356-0729-1)

© 2016 Birkhäuser Verlag GmbH, Basel
P.O. Box 44, 4009 Basel, Switzerland
Part of Walter de Gruyter GmbH, Berlin/Boston
and Bauverlag BV GmbH, Gütersloh, Berlin

bau|| ||**verlag**

Printed on acid-free paper produced from chlorine-free pulp. TCF ∞
Printed in Germany

ISBN 978-3-0356-0848-9

9 8 7 6 5 4 3 2 1

www.birkhauser.com

Contents

Anthropology of the City

Prologue

Howard S. Becker

Learning to Observe in Chicago

I am reading Jean Peneff's[1] account of the observational experiences of his generation in a small town in Southwestern France after WWII. He describes how the kids could watch the tradesmen at work in the street, because most workshops were not big enough to hold all the things the artisans did; how these workers would have the kids help them ("Hold this, kid!") or send them on errands ("Go get me this or that tool" or "Go get me a beer from the tavern"). He talks about watching the dealings, honest and not so honest, of the farmers as they bought and sold cattle and horses, and of watching and seeing how some of them put the money from their sale in their wallet and went home while others went off to the tavern and drank it up. He talks about how the kids knew all about the adulterous affairs which were not so uncommon in the town. He says that experiences like these gave the kids the taste for observation and some real experience with, and skill in, observing. A good skill for a would-be sociologist.

When I was a kid in Chicago, I had some similar experiences. Of course, we didn't have a lot of people working at their trades in the street where they were easy for us kids to observe. But we had some other things.

The El. When I was perhaps ten, my boy friends and I would take advantage of the structure of the Chicago elevated train system (the El, everyone called it that) to pay one fare and ride all day long. Our mothers would pack us a sandwich and we would walk a few blocks to Lake Street, where the Lake Street El line ran from our neighborhood on the far West Side of the city to the Loop, the downtown center (so-called because it was ringed by the elevated lines, all of which converged from every part of the city on this center, went around it, and back to where they had come from). Once you got on a train, you could find places where the lines crossed – especially in the Loop – and change to another train that went to another part of the city. Six or seven major lines ran to the three main parts of the city and, Chicago being a very large city, they went a long way.

So, for example, we could ride the Lake Street El from our neighborhood, nearly at the end of that line, to downtown, transfer to the Jackson Park line, which went to the South Side, and ride 6 or 7 miles to the end of that line at Stony Island Avenue, walk across the platform and take the same train back to the center, where we could transfer to a North Side Rogers Park train and ride that to Howard Street. And do that all day long, covering the entire city, before we went home, tired and happy. What did we see? We saw the buildings and how they varied from place to place: the poor deteriorating wooden apartment buildings in the city's poorer neighborhoods; the multi-story brick buildings in neighborhoods that were more well to do; the one-family houses of some ethnic neighborhoods; and so on. We learned the characteristic ethnic patterns of the city by reading the signs on the businesses we went by and learned that the Poles lived on Milwaukee Avenue, the Italians on the Near West Side, the Swedes farther north, the Blacks on the South Side, and so on. We saw people of different racial and ethnic groups as they got on and off the train, and learned who lived where (we were very good at reading ethnicity from small clues, including listening to the languages spoken, styles of clothing, even the smell of the food people carried).

We saw the industrial parts of the city: the factories and the buildings that housed them, the lines of trucks that served them. We saw the railroad yards that served the city; Chicago was the major railroad hub of the country. We saw the thriving neighborhood shopping centers and the kinds of stores that were there.

We saw things close up as well as from a distance. As all these people got on and off the cars we rode in, we knew we were different from many of them – racially different, different in class, different in ethnicity. We knew that we were Jewish and lots of these people weren't; we weren't always sure what to make of that but we thought it was probably just as well if the others didn't know it.

In many of the places the trains went through, the buildings were very close to the tracks, maybe no more than five feet away, and the windows in the buildings looked out directly on to the tracks. So we could look into people's apartments and watch them going about the ordinary routines of apartment living: making and eating meals, cleaning, doing laundry, sitting around listening to the radio and drinking coffee, women doing each other's hair, kids playing. We seldom saw anything private – people having sex – but we sometimes saw women who weren't fully dressed and that excited us, it wasn't something a ten- or eleven-year-old boy saw very often. This gave us a lot of material on differing ways of life to think about.

As we rode we observed, looking closely at everything that went by our little window on the city, commenting to each other about what we saw, seeing the differences and taking them home with us to think about. By the time I was, say, twelve, I had a good understanding of the physical and social structure of the city, at least from a geographic point of view.

Notes

1   Editorial note: Jean Peneff is a French sociologist, who among others introduced the Chicago School of Sociology to France. This prologue has originally been written for his book *Le goût de l'observation* (Paris : La Découverte, 2009).

Introduction

In this book you will become acquainted with some remarkable people: Marta from Detroit, Curtis from Chicago Woodlawn, Mick from south London and Tarek from Berlin Tempelhof. Anthropologists hung around with them, spoke with them, argued with them, laughed with them, drove around with them, invited them to their homes. And wrote down their stories …

The first part of the book *(Anthropology in the City)* offers three examples of ethnographic studies in London, Detroit and Berlin, following up on Peter Jackson's classic introduction to urban ethnography. These studies by Les Back, Ruth Behar and Moritz Ege provide first-hand observations of lower class communities and let them speak for themselves. They show how city life is guided by a "structure of feeling", i.e. by a sense of togetherness that is expressed and realized through symbols, gestures, music, fashion, accessories and tattoos. The neighbourhood serves as a refuge from the stigmas of society outside, it also serves as a source of pride. These studies are in line with the general interest of Urban Anthropology: since the days of the Chicago School of Sociology, which some consider as the birthplace of Urban Anthropology, the underside of city life has been the most prominent subject of inquiry. As Peter Jackson in this volume put it, "the subjects of ethnographic research have tended to be the poor and relatively powerless residents of multiethnic inner-city areas" (33). Chicago School classics include Nels Anderson's study of *The Hobo* (1923), F.M. Thrasher's *The Gang* (1927), Louis Wirth's *The Ghetto* (1928) and Paul Cressey's *The Taxi-Dance Hall* (1932). The *second generation* of Chicago School research equally studied gangs, street culture and urban underdogs, among them Elliott Liebow's study of black streetcorner men in Washington, D.C. named *Tally's Corner* (1967), and Elijah Anderson's *A Place on the Corner* (1976). Ulf Hannerz' Soulside (1968), though not originating from Chicago School, provides another example of ghetto ethnography of this time. Sometimes criticized for exoticizing urban culture, these ethnographies, too, reported on poor inner-city communities and their struggle to maintain a living. Up until today, urban ethnography has continued to return to other social worlds in order to understand the diversity of city life.

Equally, the methodology of urban ethnography is and always has been urban fieldwork: the observation of people in situ. Through participation and observation, the researcher seeks to acquaint him- or herself with the discrete circumstances of urban society. He or she gets up close, conducting his or her life in face-to-face proximity to the persons and circumstances under study for a significant period of time. It then becomes possible for research reports to provide the kind of description and quotation that moves the reader *inside* the world under study. Fieldwork is about *being there,* a motivated relocation, where the anthropologist (from the middle class) seeks "to penetrate and interpret social worlds apparently quite alien from their own" (22).

The studies of Back, Behar and Ege of contemporary urban culture are not directly related to the Chicago School. Rather, they explicitly or implicitly pick up on the subject and develop their own take on lower class urban neighbourhood within the framework of their time and place. Influenced by British Cultural Studies (28), the British sociologist Back and the German European Ethnologist Ege put pop and popular culture at the centre of urban ethnography. They observe and report how problems of social inequality and despair are faced up to and experienced through a "structure of feeling" that is formed in the ephemeral sphere of fashion and style. In recent years, in which European socioeconomic forces and the impact of a neoliberalizing welfare state have made the fault lines of social inequality increasingly visible, the interest in the underside of city life has increased evermore. With the triumph of popular culture, social inequality is increasingly acted out and lived through within a mass market of products and images, that people appropriate in order to make sense of their everyday lives. Strategies of individual style and fashion do not change the larger economic and social structures, but make them liveable and challengeable. These contemporary ethnographies are in line with the Chicago School tradition of hanging around in "places of cigarettes, hamburgers and tattoos", as Back puts it, and "portraying the sights and sounds of urban life" (23).

Furthermore, the authors offer insights into their fieldwork methodology. Behar and Back make exciting methodological suggestions, pointing to urban ethnography at the beginning of the 21st century: they include the ethnography of one's own family in order to understand in fuller detail the wider society in which researchers and the subjects of their research are equally embedded. It makes us aware of the fact that within urban settings, anthropology does not deal with cultures *out there* (as the case with classic, non-Western anthropology), but with our next-door neighbours. The ethnographers' lives are not disconnected from the environment around them, but socially interlinked and emotionally entangled. These entanglements, Behar suggests, should be faced up front. They are not an obstacle to objectivity. Rather, highlighting these entanglements and being open about one's emotions as a fieldworker help to clarify the larger forces of society that drive our emotions and our thinking.

Peter Jackson's essay "Urban Ethnography", which frames the first part of the book, was written in 1985. As he mentions, in the 1980s, there developed a new way of thinking and theorising the city, the *Anthropology of the City,* which became an important line of thinking in the last two decades and which is the subject of the second part of the book.

The second part of the book introduces *Anthropology of the City.* Rather than studying the everyday life of a particular neighbourhood, *Anthropology of the City* refers to the city as a whole: the ways people and communities perceive and make sense of the city. Under scrutiny are the images and sensations that are produced by cities at large such as Berlin, London or New York and how they are felt and lived. *Imaginaire,* as Lindner points out, reaches back to the French tradition of addressing questions of "mentalité" and "mémoire collective" (114). It is the European city that stimulates this concept of the urban imaginary: with its ancient urban nuclei and its historical layers reaching back to the Middle Ages, unlike US American cities. This concept was born out of a sense of loss and nostalgia, ever since modern city planning destroyed old and established city structures, starting with the industrial revolution in the 19th century, followed by the functional city planning of the 1950s and the sanitizing of the urban environment since the 1980s.

This approach was formalised in 1980, when Swedish anthropologist Ulf Hannerz suggested the study of anthropology *of* the city rather than *in* the city.[1] This was at a time when the deindustrialization of the Western city was more or less complete. Entertainment, urban festivals and the service industry began to mould the urban landscape. Questions of security and control and how they can be secured through urban design started to occupy the minds of politicians and urban planners. This development was accompanied by the discovery of the *Creative City* as location factor. Various European cities started to work on individual city branding in order to express the unique quality of their city and thus redirect global flows of tourists and money. The discovery of *Anthropology of Cities* is part of this urban renaissance and its critical companion. As Jonathan Raban criticizes: behind all strategies of urban planning, "lie a savage contempt for the city and an arrogant desire to refashion human society into almost any shape other than the one we have at present" (133).

In German-speaking countries, Rolf Lindner is among the advocates of the imaginary of the city. He argues that the city resists visions of urban planners and city politics. It is moulded by larger forces such as economy, social structure and morphology. Thus, the imaginary of the city develops beyond or below their control. Sometimes criticized as homogenized urban spaces, London, Berlin, Paris and other cities are actually living beings that do have distinct personalities.

To sum it up: whereas *Anthropology in the City* refers to a particular research practice, i.e. urban ethnography or fieldwork, *Anthropology of the City* refers to a programmatic approach to the city, that shares an ethnographic sensibility without necessarily conducting fieldwork in the city. Whereas *Anthropology in the City* is clearly located within the discipline of anthropology and qualitative sociology, *Anthropology of the City* is interdisciplinary, blurring the boundaries between social science, humanities, art and architecture. Whereas *Anthropology in the City* originated in the US-American Chicago School of Sociology, *Anthropology of the City* originated from Europe. It aims at locating the subjects of urban ethnographies in terms of their larger social and historical context and also in terms of the built environment and the urban landscape. There is an academic debate about whether and how these two approaches are connected, but so far the study suggests that one cannot talk about *Anthropology of Cities* without talking about *Anthropology in Cities*.

It is by the very nature of the city that its imaginary can only be grasped with an interdisciplinary approach that embraces storytelling, literature and journalism. Thus, in the second part of the anthology, the line between the fields has been blurred. It includes writers from various fields beyond anthropology, i.e. sociology, architecture and literature. Despite the variety of approaches, all authors share an interest in the question of how the city is experienced on a street-level. The authors sympathize with what some might criticize as *magazine sociology*: theorising on cities in a cosmopolitan, urban style. Adapting poetic approaches to the city does not contradict the search for objective patterns and rules of urban life, rather, it deepens the understanding of it.

Besides the urban imaginary, the *Anthropology of Cities* also questions urban living, the way people act, behave and perform in public spaces. As British travel writer Jonathan Raban has put it: what is special about behaviour in urban public arenas? How do people behave in restaurants, late night tube trains, certain streets and squares? What makes their behavior distinct from the small city? Implicitly referring to Georg Simmel's classic "Die Großstädte und das Geistesleben" ("The metropolis and mental life"), Raban explains that in a city of strangers, where people generally do not know each other, citizens tend to put on a show in order to escape the anonymous mass. People use fashion and style to give themselves "cartoon-like outlines", easy to read by the people who live in cities and who are *in the know*. "Synecdoche", as Raban calls it, "is much more than a rhetorical figure, it is a means of survival" (135). It is challenging to compare Raban's thoughts with the ethnographic studies of Back, Behar and Ege. The way Back describes the meaning of tattoos, for example, as designs that are a "continuous part of personality" (Raban) that condense and communicate emotions and sympathies. "Impression management" (101), as Ege explains, should not be trivialized, because it has an empowering quality and gives a sense of solidarity and belonging to the neighbourhood and beyond.

Raban has written a flaming apology for street life and spectacle. In 1980, when he wrote this essay, the prejudices towards the city as a place of crime and vice were stronger than today, in the city of the festival. But many urban neighbourhoods still struggle with the anonymous atmosphere created by modernist housing projects from the 1950s onwards. As Zardini put it, the "death of the street" is virulent – more than ever before – due to the sanitization of the urban environment for the sake of security and control. Just as Raban, he highlights the importance of street life and its experiential qualities vis-à-vis the functional and sanitized city. He criticizes the ocular-centrism of city planners and architects and invites urban researchers and city planners to consider the sensual qualities of city life, landscape, soundscape and smellscape. We are in need of a sensual understanding, being in the world through the body, because, as Zardini puts it, the cities are "places of our bodies and souls" (149).

The closing essay by Loïc Wacquant provides connections between *Anthropology in the City* and the *Anthropology of the City* – Wacquant combines both a European and an American way of thinking. He got his PhD at the department of sociology of the University of Chicago, but started his academic career at a French university. His most well-known ethnographic study, *Body and Soul* (2004), is about a black urban boxing gym in Chicago. In his essay, he undertakes a "ride-along", as Kusenbach in this volume puts it (156), through the very neighbourhood of the boxing gym with his friend Curtis, who in a stream of consciousness reflects about the environment. The car ride is not only a trip through the streets, it is also a – very sad – journey into the psyche of an urban underclass. Like Lindner, Wacquant picks up on Maurice Halbwachs' notion of "mémoire collective". The desolated area mirrors the people's conditions and becomes tangible – a physical manifestation of their state of mind. People in this neighbourhood are neglected by the neoliberal system and experience this loss through the urban landscape. Thus, the images and symbols of the urban landscape – closed down shops, decaying buildings and dirt – is acting upon the people and vice versa. How Wacquant puts it: there is a "link between the built environment, social structure, and collective psychology" (165).

The method of data-collection Wacquant uses is what the sociologist Margarethe Kusenbach has called "go-along". This practice implicitly echoes artistic movements of the 1920s and 1930s, at times when Surrealists undertook "déambulations" in Paris in order to uncover the hidden side of city life. In the 1950s, the French writer Guy Debord (part of the artist group "Situationist International") promoted "dérive" as a technique to explore the relation between the psyche and the built environment, i.e. the psychogeography of the city. Nowadays, with the festivalization of the urban environment, the urban imaginary becomes a tool of city planning. The go-along, as Wacquant has shown, is a means to experience everyday urbanism on a street-level.

The encounter between the researcher and the subject of research is a very personal expierence. Comic-strips by the artist Nele Brönner comment on these encounters. These *true fictions* – invented stories rooted in actual events – show Back, Ege, Behar, Lindner, Raban and Wacquant conducting field research. They are the results of e-mail-exchanges between the artist and the authors, in order to grasp a significant moment of their fieldwork and transform it into a story. They not only highlight and illustrate the fieldresearch experience, but take ethnographic work further by showing the dramatic and poetic qualities of being out in the field. Inspired by Lindner's essay "Die Angst des Forschers vor dem Feld"[2] ('The researcher's fear of the field'), they dramatise the encounter between the fieldresearcher and his or her subject as a moment of sympathy, fear, misunderstanding, humour and embarrassment. Urban Anthropology, even though it is an academic discipline, is built upon personal encounters that are nothing but human and sometimes funny.

Urban Anthropology has become a key discipline in exploring contemporary society in general and the culture of cities in particular. Together with Psychology and cultural Marxism, Anthropology is a fundamental discourse of modernity. What does Urban Anthropology and Sensing the City mean? It means cultivating a sensibility towards the city, its people and its structures of feeling. It means to open the senses towards the atmosphere of the urban landscape and the symbols, images and legends that are shaped by it. It means hanging around in the city and finding friends. As Robert Ezra Park, the *spiritus rector* of the Chicago School, in an often quoted instruction for his students put it: "Go into the district, get the feeling, become acquainted with people."[3]

In August 2015, Anja Schwanhäußer

Notes

1 Ulf Hannerz: Exploring the City. Inquiries toward an Urban Anthropology. Columbia University Press: New York, Chichester, West Sussex, 1980, S. 3. See Jackson in this volume: 35.

2 Lindner, Rolf. "Die Angst des Forschers vor dem Feld. Überlegungen zur teilnehmenden Beobachtung als Interaktionsprozess." From *Zeitschrift für Volkskunde 77*, 1981.

3 Robert E. Park, quoted from Rolf Lindner. *The reportage of urban culture. Robert Park and the Chicago School.* Cambridge: Cambridge University Press, 1996. Originally published in German as *Die Entdeckung der Stadtkultur. Soziologie aus der Erfahrung der Reportage.* Frankfurt am Main: Suhrkamp 1990: 10.

Anthropology in the City

Peter Jackson

Urban Ethnography

A marked revival of interest in ethnographic research has taken place among social anthropologists and urban sociologists in recent years (e.g. Hannerz 1980; Burgess 1982; Hammersley and Atkinson 1983; Ellen 1984) which is beginning to claim the attention of geographers (e.g. Jackson and Smith 1984).[1] Interest is already sufficient across the social sciences to sustain a journal devoted entirely to urban ethnography, defined to include those studies which employ participant observation and intensive qualitative interviewing 'to convey the inner life and texture of the diverse social enclaves and personal circumstances of urban societies' *(Urban Life)*.

A comprehensive review of urban ethnography is not possible here and our horizons must necessarily be narrowed. The present paper is therefore deliberately selective and concentrates on certain themes and issues raised by the literature of urban 'community studies'. This emphasis on the urban is problematic as several recent authors (notably Saunders 1981) have pointed out. What is specifically 'urban' about the community studies which we are to review apart from their location? And what can the ethnographer contribute to a workable theory of urbanism?

In making the transition to urban research, anthropologists have discovered that their traditional methods of year-round isolation from their own ordinary lives and round-the-clock participation in the ordinary lives of other people are no longer possible. They have been obliged to devise new research strategies that are feasible in dense urban settings and to ask, as one anthropologist has put it: 'is it possible to map context without sitting in the middle of it?' (Wallman 1984: 42). Geographers are now asking themselves the same questions and, while further elaboration of these points is mainly confined to the conclusion, their significance is implicit throughout the paper.

Besides a preoccupation with the urban, this review also concentrates on studies which employ some version of participant observation rather than qualitative interviewing or other research strategies which may be more familiar to geographers (cf. Jackson 1983a). Questions of theory and method are raised which transcend traditional disciplinary boundaries. Yet the geographer can take solace from Janowitz's magisterial survey of recent sociological research on the residential community which he sees as embodying a distinctively 'geographical dimension' (Janowitz 1978).

Within this general framework, a number of specific topics are selected for comment including some observations on the relationship between ethnography and theory; an evaluation of the ethnographer's contribution to the literature on ethnicity, class and politics; and a discussion of ethnography as method. The paper begins, though, by considering the intellectual roots of ethnographic research on the city which have continued to exert a powerful influence on current work.

1 Intellectual Origins: The 'Chicago school'

The urban sociologists of the 'Chicago school' are well known to geographers for their studies of the city's human ecology (e.g. Park and Burgess 1925). Their morphological studies of the growth of the city according to ecological processes of 'invasion' and 'succession' have been celebrated as the forerunners of social area analysis and factorial ecology, while Park's interest in social and physical distance has been heralded as the original inspiration for much contemporary work in 'spatial sociology' (Peach 1975).

In recent years, however, geographers and sociologists have shown a growing hostility to the 'Chicago school' authors for their tacit Social Darwinism and for their uncritical stance towards the specific conditions of *laissez-faire* capitalism which produced the distinctive form of the city which they regarded as a universal 'natural order'. Following his critique of the 'reactionary and ideological character' of Louis Wirth's writings about urbanism (Castells 1976), for example, Castells went on to dismiss the whole corpus of Chicago sociology as dedicated to the 'myth of urban culture' (Castells 1977). Harvey has been equally critical of the 'culturalist' explanations of Park and Burgess (Harvey 1973), while humanists like David Ley have also found fault with the reductionist view of urban sociology as 'social physics' which they attribute to Park (Ley 1980). Geographers have apparently chosen to ignore the rival interpretation of Park's work as being 'on the side of *verstehen* sociology as opposed to positivistic approaches' (Turner 1967: xx), although there are recent signs that this balance is being redressed (Entrikin 1980; Jackson and Smith 1981; 1984).

The non-positivistic version of 'Chicago school' sociology is most readily sustained by an examination of their pioneering contributions to urban ethnography. These studies were carried out as doctoral and masters' dissertations by graduate students in the Department of Sociology at Chicago during the 1920s and 1930s. Several were later published by the University of Chicago Press. (The dissertations are listed in an appendix to Faris 1967; the monographs are sympathetically reviewed by Hannerz 1980). A series of richly descriptive vignettes resulted from the students' attempts to gain firsthand acquaintance with their subject matter following the instructions of their mentor, Robert Park.

It is possible to discern a number of common themes in these diverse ethnographies which reveal their intellectual roots and highlight their unique contribution. Each of the monographs attempts to present a faithful and sympathetic portrait of the social and moral order which lies behind the outward signs of an apparently alien and 'disorganized' world (cf. Jackson 1984). This is as true of Anderson's classic evocation of the world of *The hobo* (Anderson 1923) as it is of Cressey's description of *The taxi-dance hall* (Cressey 1932). Each draws intellectual sustenance from the pragmatic philosophy which inspired Park through his reading of William James, John Dewey and, to a lesser extent perhaps, also George Herbert Mead (cf. Smith 1984a). From James, Park learned not to be blind to the world of other people but to seek to capture 'the zest, the tingle, the excitement of reality' as conveyed by first-hand 'acquaintance with' their various worlds (James 1899). From Dewey, Park derived his faith in the role of human communication as a means to greater knowledge and mutual understanding (Park 1940), underscoring his earliest conception of the sociologist as a kind of super-reporter (Park 1950). And from Mead, Park gained his view of society as an emergent and dynamic system in which meaning and identity are constantly negotiated through interaction (Mead 1934).

Two further influences on the early 'Chicago school' sociologists should also be acknowledged: from his friend and colleague in Chicago, W. I. Thomas, Park inherited a series of concepts (including 'disorganization' and 'definition of the situation') and a set of methods (including the use of personal documents) which were used to structure countless ethnographies (cf. Janowitz 1966).[2] And from the formal sociology of Georg Simmel, Park developed a characteristic interest in social forms including that most celebrated 'social type', the stranger (Simmel 1908). Simmel's influence has been particularly strong and provides a thread of continuity between several generations of ethnographers who acknowledge implicit allegiance to a generally 'understated' interactionist sociology (Rock 1979).[3] Park himself, for example, was fascinated by city life, having witnessed the phenomenal growth of metropolitan Chicago in the early years of this century (cf. Mayer and Wade 1969). In Park's words:

> The social problem is fundamentally a city problem. It is the problem of achieving in the freedom of the city a social order and a social control equivalent to that which grew up naturally in the family, the clan, and the tribe (Park 1929; reprinted in Park 1952: 74).

His inspiration, here as elsewhere, however, was Simmel rather than Tönnies. It was Park's student, Louis Wirth, who in 1925 cited Simmel's essay on 'The metropolis and mental life' (Simmel 1903) as 'the most important single article on the city from the sociological point of view' (Wirth 1925: 219).

Simmel's essay on 'The stranger' (Simmel 1908) had an even more pervasive and lasting influence. It is explicitly cited in Anderson's study of *The hobo* (Anderson 1923) and is an implicit reference in Wirth's study of *The ghetto* (Wirth 1928). It was taken up by Everett Stonequist in his analysis of *The marginal man* (Stonequist 1937) and by Norman Hayner in his study of *Hotel life* (Hayner 1936). This intellectual genealogy is traced in detail by Donald Levine (1979). Combined with his seminal ideas about the positive role of conflict as an integrative social force (Simmel 1955), Simmel's influence on contemporary urban sociology and on urban ethnography in particular can scarcely be exaggerated.

Rather than continue to treat in generalities, however, the argument is best pursued by more detailed analysis of specific ethnographies. It will be convenient to select two studies from the first generation of 'Chicago ethnography' and to trace their counterparts in more recent literature. It will also then be possible to review the contribution of other early ethnographic studies which fall outside the direct influence of the 'Chicago school'.

II The Chicago School Inheritance

Louis Wirth's classic study of the ghetto (Wirth 1928) is particularly deserving of comment because of its many points of divergence from the ethnographic tradition established by his teachers and colleagues at Chicago. Although Wirth tells us that his study originated in an investigation of the ghetto district of Chicago, it rapidly developed beyond the study of a particular geographical area to involve an examination of 'the natural history of an institution and the psychology of a people' (Wirth 1928: xi). The 'natural history' extends for more than one thousand years but focuses on one particular old world ghetto (Frankfurt). Although he shares with other Chicago ethnographers the stylistic device of lengthy quotations from primary and secondary material, his analysis diverges from the ethnographic tradition in several respects. Wirth is more willing than most ethnographers to speak of universal truths ('human nature', 'fundamental motives' etc.). He is firm in his opinion that assimilation is an inevitable prospect for the Jews as for other ethnic groups in America; the ghetto is a transitional stage between the old world and the new which can only be preserved as a physical entity by renewed immigration (Wirth 1928: 127–28). He also adopts a more evaluative stance towards his subjects than is common among other ethnographers: the ghetto community lacks 'breadth and substance', is the slave of 'tradition and sentiment', 'shallow in content and out of touch with the world' (Wirth 1928: 226). As a result, his ethnography lacks the immediacy and power of evocation which more sympathetic observers manage to achieve. Only in his description of the Maxwell Street market (Wirth 1928: 231–40) and perhaps also in his account of 'Deutschland', the Lawndale area of second settlement (Wirth 1928: 245–61), does Wirth's ethnography truly come to life. Nonetheless, his work has inspired frequent emulation although social historians have been less prone to cite his work than have urban sociologists (cf. Osofsky 1963; Spear 1967; with Drake and Cayton 1945; Suttles 1968).

Thrasher's classic ethnography of the gang (Thrasher 1927) is also worthy of our close attention because of the significance which he attached to the territorial dimension. On the basis of seven years' fieldwork and data collection, including the amassing of over 250 personal documents, Thrasher argued that gang conflict was particularly concentrated in areas which had undergone rapid racial transition or which were currently on the fringe of the expanding 'black belt'. These areas were interstitial in both a geographical and social sense (Thrasher 1927: 20).

Although Thrasher drew on a suite of concepts from 'Chicago school' theory (including the notion of invasion/succession, natural history, disorganization, definition of the situation, and universe of discourse) much of the book is essentially descriptive and taxonomic rather than analytic. He was far from explicit about his methods which have been described as 'unsystematic and incomplete in essential details' (Short 1963). For all that, many subsequent theorists have built on his original interpretation of gang behaviour as a means of finding a substitute for what conventional society fails to provide: 'a spontaneous attempt on the part of boys to create a society of their own where none adequate to their needs exists' (Thrasher 1927: 268). Several classic theories of delinquency have built on these foundations (e.g. Cohen 1955; Cloward and Ohlin 1960), concurring with Thrasher's conclusion that gang membership offers a means of acquiring status where more conventional routes to recognition and prestige are currently denied. Geographers have also attempted to extend Thrasher's work, particularly concerning the role of proximity in increasing aggression and in terms of the territorial aspects of his ideas in general (e.g. Ley 1974; Ley and Cybriwsky 1974).

Among the 'second generation' of urban ethnographers, Liebow's (1967) study of black streetcorner men in Washington, D.C., is an excellent illustration of both the strengths and weaknesses of the ethnographic approach, drawing on the heritage of Chicago sociology and extending it in several respects. Its principal strength lies in its very vivid evocation of a particular urban milieu and of a group of people of radically different social background from the author. Liebow's study captures the reality of everyday life for a group of streetcorner men as they search for work, share their leisure time together and reflect on their common experience as husbands, lovers and friends. His achievement as a white, middle-class graduate student in successfully establishing the respect and friendship of a group of black streetcorner men should not be underestimated. Together with a handful of other ethnographers like Hannerz (1969) and Ley (1974), he bears witness to the potential for social scientists to penetrate and interpret social worlds apparently quite alien from their own.

Building on the Chicago ethnographers' tradition of relevance to social policy, Liebow's book includes some sharp criticisms of current thinking on the relationship between poverty, family life and childrearing among low-income blacks. But as with so many ethnographies, there is an obvious reluctance to generalize from the particular to any broader theoretical conclusions. This is most apparent in the relative absence of references to other research on the sociology of family life, urban poverty and race. Apart from tacit references to W.I. Thomas's 'definition of the situation', there is no explicit discussion of the intellectual context in which this particular ethnography was produced. Current research on juvenile delinquency is acknowledged together with some discussion of the controversy generated by the Moynihan Report, but only Whyte and Gans are singled out in footnotes from the vast sociological tradition with which Liebow's study bears comparison. His highest order of abstraction concerns behaviour at the interpersonal level as in his interesting discussion of pseudo-kin relations ('going for brothers'). But the study cries out for more explicit theoretical analysis.

More recent studies in this tradition betray similar weaknesses. Elijah Anderson's ethnography of Jelly's bar and liquor store in Chicago's South Side (Anderson 1976) succeeds as well as Liebow or Hannerz in portraying the sights and sounds of urban life, but there is little attempt to locate his particular findings in terms of a broader theoretical or social context. This is a recurrent criticism of urban ethnography and a theme to which we will return.

III Independent Invention?

While it is possible to trace the intellectual genealogy of books like *Tally corner* and *Soulside* back to the original inspiration of the 'Chicago school' authors and forward to more recent studies, such as that by Anderson (1976), other classic studies in urban ethnography evince much greater independence from the tradition established at Chicago. Whyte's *Street corner society* (1955), for example, was undertaken from Harvard, although as Suttles (1976) points out, Chicago insisted on giving him a PhD for it and on publishing it through their University Press. The classic studies of Muncie, Indiana by Robert and Helen Lynd (1929; 1937) are even more relevant here, not least because of their contemporaneity with the work of Park's colleagues and students at Chicago. However, their links with the 'Chicago school' were tenuous indeed. Between the completion of *Middletown* (1929) and *Middletown in transition* (1937), Robert Lynd was appointed to Franklin Giddings's chair of sociology at Columbia University in New York. Coincidentally, Florian Znaniecki spent some time at Columbia in the early 1930s as a visiting professor giving Lynd his only close contact with the 'Chicago school'. Znaniecki's influence on the second Middletown study, which is more sophisticated both theoretically and methodologically than its predecessor, remains a matter for speculation (Madge 1962).

The Middletown studies are of interest in the present context not only because they 'set the style for future community studies' (Bell and Newby 1971: 82) but also because they raise fascinating questions of comparison with contemporary ethnographic research in Chicago. For example, Robert Park's aim of studying the city by employing 'the same patient methods of observation' as the anthropologist (Park 1952: 15) is well known. While Park looked to Franz Boas and Robert Lowie, however, the Lynds looked to Clark Wissler and W. H. R. Rivers, deriving the organizational framework for their monographs from the latter. The original Middletown volume set out to study contemporary American culture in a 'typical' small town community. (Muncie had a population of 35 000 in 1924.) The Lynds employed a range of techniques but prominent among them was participant observation during their 18 months fieldwork in the town. Historical data were employed to establish a base line in 1890 from which to explore recent changes. In this respect, the study can even be interpreted as an attempt to trace the effects of industrialization on community life (cf. Stein 1964). But as usual with ethnographic work, this broader design tends to get lost in the devotion to empirical data. In fact, the original aim of the Middletown study was to investigate religious practices and provision, but a more comprehensive study was perhaps inevitable given the functionalist assumptions then prevalent throughout the social sciences. These same assumptions encouraged the Lynds to collect the most detailed observations on all aspects of Middletown life. Indeed, it is the wealth of descriptive material for which the Middletown studies are justly famous. It is much harder to appreciate the 'crucial sociological generalizations' that other critics have discerned (cf. Stein 1964).

Middletown in transition is much more focused than the earlier study, seeking to trace the effects of economic depression on the community life of small-town America. There is also more emphasis on the analysis of power in the second volume, particularly concerning the way in which the most wealthy manufacturing family in Muncie was able to legitimate its preeminent position. While the Middletown series is still taken as a classic example of the potential for replication studies in sociological research, the quality of their ethnography is such that subsequent workers have been able to reinterpret the original findings from quite different theoretical perspectives (e.g. Polsky 1963). There is now even greater scope for assessing the potential cumulativity of ethnographic research in the

Middletown case as a second restudy has recently been published (Caplow *et al.* 1982). This third volume in the history of Middletown is again more narrowly focused than its predecessors, concentrating exclusively on aspects of family life, although further volumes are promised including a comprehensive final report. Perhaps the most striking feature of this most recent Middletown enterprise is the lavish scale of current sociological undertakings. The study employed four principal research associates and 25 research assistants to carry out 13 'major surveys'. In the course of their work, a Center for Middletown Studies was established at Ball State University.

The Middletown restudy is not, however, a unique example of replication research. Similar exercises include restudies of *The Gold Coast and the slum* (Hunter 1983) and of *The jack-roller* (Snodgrass 1982). While one might conclude optimistically about the potential value of ethnography for the study of social change, it is also possible to argue that these studies show ethnography to be an essentially synchronic method. Several studies of the same location at different points in time tend simply to produce a series of cross-sections rather than a revealing analysis of processes of change.

In this context, too, Lloyd Warner's 'Yankee City' series (originally produced as five volumes between 1941 and 1959, abridged in one volume in 1963) has frequently been criticized for its insensitivity to change. Warner conducted five years fieldwork in Newburyport, Massachusetts between 1930 and 1935 with a 30-member research staff. His links with Chicago sociology were even more remote than the Lynds. (The fieldwork for Yankee City employed students from Harvard, where Warner himself was based; the analysis was undertaken by graduate students at Chicago.) There are, however, a number of intellectual parallels with other early ethnographic endeavours. Warner had himself spent three years conducting anthropological fieldwork among Australian aborigines and readily acknowledged the inspiration of Radcliffe-Brown, Robert Lowie and Bronislaw Malinowski. Warner shares with his functionalist forebears a largely ahistorical approach, avowedly ignoring earlier research on Yankee City. While there is still a general commitment to studying the urban community 'in the round', each volume in the series focuses on class as the major analytical variable, although some books are more clearly focused than others. Stein (1964), for example, makes a good case for *The social system of the modern factory* (Warner and Low 1947) which he argues is more successful than other volumes because it seeks to explain a series of unique events (a strike) in one factory and their consequences for community life in terms of the breakdown of Yankee City's craft system through the processes of increasing bureaucratization. Balancing the particular and the general has been a persistent problem for urban ethnography, raising a number of important theoretical questions.

IV Ethnography and Theory

In a spirited defence of ethnographic research, Gerald Suttles has argued that this overwhelmingly inductive subfield has served to keep the abstract conceptual content of sociology firmly in touch with the available world of empirical observation (Suttles 1976). Suttles proceeds to define the ethnographer's role as mediating between situational and normative accounts, although the tendency in most studies has been to focus on the former rather than on the latter.[4]

The tension between ethnography and theory has been characterized for members of the 'Chicago school' as a tendency to generalize towards process rather than towards structure (cf. Turner 1967; Jackson and Smith 1981; 1984). 'Succession', 'disorganization' and 'adaptation' were stressed rather than stratification, inequality or power. But as Smith has argued, it is inherent in all experiential and participatory research strategies for the analyst to begin by making generalizations about process based on a constant stream of experience, observation, reflection and selection; only then is it possible for the analyst to make generalizations at higher levels of abstraction in terms of structure (Smith 1981).

Other ethnographers have been no less reluctant to treat structural issues. William Foote Whyte's claim to observe 'social structure in action' through participant observation (Whyte 1955: 318–19) is little more than a rhetorical device inasmuch as he was able to observe the impact of group structure on the individual. The 'Yankee City' studies (Warner 1963) also evince more concern with processes of social stratification than with the structures of inequality *per se,* and with the subjective experience of status and class rather than with their material foundation.

The charge that ethnography is atheoretic is often accompanied by the criticism that such studies are devoid of adequate historical and social context. Thus Stephen Steinberg is not alone in arguing that:

The ethnic literature abounds with community studies that explore the uniqueness and complexities of ethnic life. As a rule, however, these studies go too far in treating ethnic communities as 'worlds unto themselves', and tend to gloss over the extent to which these communities are integrated into and dependent upon the institutions of the surrounding society (Steinberg 1981: 53).

All too often, ethnographies are presented as static, cross-sectional accounts. An initial response would be to suggest that ethnographic studies should be more adequately situated in terms of their broader historical and social context. This is a minimum requirement if such works are to avoid seeming utterly static and artificially self-contained.

Recent work has attempted to address this criticism by locating particular ethnographies in the context of broader processes of structural change. Ida Susser's study of poverty and politics in the Greenpoint-Williamsburg section of Brooklyn, New York (Susser 1982) is a case in point. Her description of the daily life of a group of working-class residents is set firmly in the context of New York City's fiscal crisis and aims to explore the constraints which these changes imposed on a particular local community. She is interested in lifestyles, values and activities as a reflection of changing political and economic conditions at both a national and local level. Susser's particular contribution is in the explicit attention which she pays to the role of the state as demonstrated in her study of the interaction between officials and clients of the welfare system. She shows how officials go far beyond their statutory roles as implementers of a neutral bureaucracy to interpret their roles as aggressive and investigative regulators of the state's largesse.

While it cannot be claimed that ethnography contributes directly to the understanding of structural change, it can make a distinctive contribution in analysing the consequences of those changes in terms of their local impact. If the fiscal crisis is to be understood as a 'directed crisis', having differential impacts on various sections of the community (Marcuse 1981), then it is clearly necessary to consider those people who bear the brunt of the costs. But one must remain sceptical about whether ethnography can improve our understanding of the structural roots of New York's fiscal crisis which lie firmly in the political economy.

Ira Katznelson approaches the issue in a different way, sketching a history of American patterns of urbanism and class before proceeding to an analysis of the local political scene in northern Manhattan (Katznelson 1981). The study goes far beyond conventional community studies both in terms of policy analysis and social theory. The author himself describes the transition from macro-historical analysis to case study as a peculiar mix (Katznelson 1981: xiv), but some such combination is surely necessary in order to capture the complex interplay of structural imperatives and human agency which are revealed in Katznelson's detailed ethnography. It is clearly an advance on traditional geographical analyses which rarely go beyond simplistic arguments about 'choice' and 'constraint'.[5]

Indeed, the structure/agency debate might be seen to offer encouragement to the ethnographer. The theory of structuration (Giddens 1979; Gregory 1981), in particular, has shown the folly of polarizing choice and constraint, and argues instead that structures are reproduced through practices which themselves perpetuate and transform those structures. The ethnographer's role might therefore be interpreted theoretically as to study the instantiation of structures in particular social practices. Susser's ethnography of the welfare system as a series of patterned interactions between officials and applicants suggests one possible model for such analyses (Susser 1982).

The Centre for Contemporary Cultural Studies at the University of Birmingham, England provides another possible model for theorizing the relationship between the social practices which constitute the material of ethnographic description and the structural forces under which these practices are produced. They analyse the actions of subordinate groups in terms of resistance to domination (see, for example, Centre for Contemporary Cultural Studies 1982; Hall and Jefferson 1976; Clarke et al. 1979). Geographers have been inspired by their example to provide a 'situated knowledge of local reality' (Burgess, in press) – a reality which can be captured through ethnographic research and situated in terms of a theoretically informed understanding of social structures.

Geographers have also shown considerable interest in Abner Cohen's recent studies of the Notting Hill Carnival which combine detailed ethnography with a penetrating theoretical analysis of the subtle interplay between politics and culture which Carnival entails (see, for example, Jackson 1983b; Jackson and Smith 1984). Cohen's analysis stresses the relatively autonomous cultural dimension of Carnival which is nonetheless structured by the political (Cohen 1980). This relationship is clarified by seeing Carnival as a contested cultural performance involving conflict and negotiation between the various groups who seek to control the development of Carnival (Cohen 1982).

Susan Smith has recently extended Cohen's analysis to argue that ethnicity is routinely 'negotiated' in everyday social interaction, not just in the ritualized display of Carnival (Smith 1984b). Her research on perceptions of crime in north central Birmingham indicates that ethnic symbols are regularly chosen as the most appropriate visible criteria for choosing between alternative strategies for managing casual traffic relationships (such as distancing and avoidance strategies). These strategies offer residents of inner-city areas some degree of control over their uncertain environment but also consciously reproduce the patterns of dominance, subordination and resistance which are inherent in the structured inequality of British society. Her account provides further evidence of the possibility of combining ethnographic detail with structural analysis, interpreting ethnicity as one means of manipulating power.

V Ethnicity, Class and Politics

One of the areas of current theoretical debate to which urban ethnography has made a distinctive contribution is in the analysis of ethnicity and class. While there has been no unitary progress towards any particular understanding, a variety of interpretations of the complex intersections between ethnicity and class has emerged. The recent ethnographic literature has also indicated one of the weaknesses of the early 'Chicago school' sociologists, namely their apparent reluctance to admit an explicitly political dimension into their discussions of ethnic succession, social mobility and neighbourhood change.

William Kornblum has provided perhaps the best analysis of the interweaving of class and ethnic allegiance in his ethnography of the mixed-ethnic steel-mill communities of South Chicago (Kornblum 1974). His study is particularly appealing in the present context not only in exploring the importance of specifically political processes in shaping intergroup conflict and adaptation, but also in demonstrating the salience of an explicitly territorial dimension to local social organization. In this, he builds on Gerald Suttles' earlier discussion of ethnicity and territory as elements in the 'ordered segmentation' of a similarly multiethnic neighbourhood on Chicago's Near West Side (Suttles 1968). But Kornblum's study differs in showing how the territorial organization of the local community is geared specifically towards the exigencies of steel production, creating a distinctive way of life in which some groups participate more easily than others. Those groups who have established a secure niche in the steel mills, like the Poles and southern Slavs, have simultaneously developed tight-knit residential communities close to their place of work. More recent arrivals, like the Mexicans and blacks, have been unable to secure a comparably solid residential base in South Chicago. This greater discontinuity between work and residence means not only a longer journey to work, but also much greater insecurity of employment. There are further repercussions in terms of political organization. Thus, the Mexicans are divided between two residential neighbourhoods (Millgate and Irondale), making any appeal to Mexican solidarity a matter of delicate negotiation. The blacks are even worse off, lacking any cohesive residential base in South Chicago despite their large numbers in the mills. The exclusionary strategies which white ethnic residents employ in their residential communities indicate their political and economic strength, perpetuated also through their informal broker's role in introducing new recruits to the complex processes of steel production.

Ethnicity is revealed as one means by which groups hang on to hard-won political and economic gains. Kornblum is adamant, however, in his refusal to treat ethnic affiliation as the mere instrumentality of class or status. That is, while status is frequently negotiated *through ethnicity*, it is never possible simply to reduce one dimension to the other. On the basis of two and a half years fieldwork in South Chicago, Kornblum rejects the interpretation of ethnic and racial politics as 'false consciousness' (Kornblum 1974: 90). In the case of the smaller ethnic groups (Jewish and Greek merchants, for example), the author shows how they seek to appeal to broader loyalties than those of the ethnic group or neighbourhood enclave. But even for the larger ethnic groups, successful participation in ward politics and labour unions demands carefully 'negotiated aggregations' among multiple dimensions of affiliation of which 'managing ethnicity' is but one vitally important strategy. In Kornblum's own words:

> [P]rimary groups are developed on multiple principles of affiliation: ethnic and neighborhood descent, common participation in a street corner gang, patronage of a local tavern, participation in precinct organizations or union caucuses, and friendships in the mills (Kornblum 1974: 21).

Recent studies have sometimes neglected this crucial point. For example, Ida Susser begins her study of poverty and politics in Brooklyn (Susser 1982) with the contention that 'conflict over neighbourhood resources can be seen as class conflict' (Susser 1982: viii). From this perspective her comments on other dimensions of social conflict are reduced to an analysis of how race and ethnicity have 'interfered with' the development of a sense of common purpose between groups. The strength of her analysis is revealed in showing the residents' success in defending tangible, material resources (such as a fire station, a senior citizens' centre or a free school lunch programme). Its weakness is in insisting that ethnicity and race have no role to play besides that of reducing working-class solidarity. The ethnographer's task might well be defined in terms of detailing the circumstances in which appeals to race or class or ethnicity are made, and evaluating the success or failure of such appeals. A presumption that certain dimensions of stratification and alliance have primacy over others is not likely to produce accurate or sensitive ethnography.

Susser's *a priori* commitment to class-based analysis is all the more surprising in view of her perceptive analysis of the distinctive role of women in neighbourhood politics. Here, Susser does not claim that gender 'interferes with' working-class solidarity, but shows the number of subtle ways in which gender and class combine in various forms of political action. The potential explanatory value of such an approach has recently been emphasized by Manuel Castells' crosscultural study of urban social movements in which the analysis proceeds from the admission that class analysis is an insufficient basis for understanding urban social change:

> [A]lthough class relationships and class struggle are fundamental in understanding the process of urban conflict, they are by no means the only or even the primary source of urban social change. Our theory must recognise other sources of urban social change: the autonomous role of the state, gender relationships, ethnic and national movements, and movements that specifically define themselves as citizen movements (Castells 1983: xviii).

More directly comparable with Susser's study of *Norman Street,* however, is Katznelson's ethnography of northern Manhattan (Katznelson 1981). Unlike Susser, Katznelson begins by asking why class is generally *absent* from the vocabulary of local discourse and why instead residents share a common language of community, ethnicity, territoriality and race (Katznelson 1981: xiv). His historical analysis shows that local politics mirror national politics in that ethnicity, territory and race have consistently been emphasized rather than class. However, he does not focus exclusively on the 'racial and ethnic fragmentation of the working class' but argues instead that 'under some circumstances, ethnic and racial ties may actually stimulate collective class activity' (Katznelson 1981: 10–11). The stage is then set for the ethnographer's analysis of *which* circumstances are favourable to such actions and which circumstances favour other modes of political expression.

Katznelson's ethnography of the Washington Heights-Inwood districts shows that internally northern Manhattan appeared to be a classless, egalitarian society (Katznelson 1981: 83). Conflicts were initially fought across an ethnic divide, between the Irish in Inwood and the Jews in Washington Heights. Later, Irish and Jewish residents found common cause in opposition to black and Hispanic newcomers. Katznelson concludes that class in American politics is largely confined to the arena of work; at home, members of the working class think of themselves as members of particular ethnic or racial groups, or simply in terms of one particular residential community or another. In Gramsci's terms, conflict is restricted to one set of 'city trenches' rather than spreading out more widely. These observations suggest a number of fruitful areas for future ethnographic work, throwing fresh light on traditional geographical notions concerning the separation of home and work, and the consequence of such a separation in terms of the ethnic division of labour (cf. Ward 1982; Harris 1984). Before geographers can begin to realize the full potential of ethnographic research, however, they must become more aware of the methodological problems which ethnography entails.

VI Ethnography as Method

In her discussions of 'humanistic method' in contemporary social geography, Susan Smith argues that such a method is characterized by its willingness to supplement participant observation with information pragmatically abstracted from documentary sources and various forms of interview (Smith 1981). Ethnographers have shown themselves to be willing to employ practically every technique available to the social scientist: sample surveys, informants, censuses, historical documents, direct participation, first-hand observations, descriptive linguistics, correlational techniques, psychological tests and so forth (Suttles 1976): 'shameless eclecticism' and 'methodological opportunism' are defining features of the ethnographer.

In a more recent paper, Smith has argued that the ethnographic methods of the 'Chicago school' were significantly extended by the greater epistemological sophistication of the anthropologists of the 'Manchester school', working out of the Rhodes-Livingstone Institute in central Africa (Smith 1984a). Whereas the ethnographic mosaic described by the Chicagoans was, in her opinion, 'riddled with inconsistencies', much greater analytical rigour was achieved by the 'Manchester school' anthropologists. This advance was attributable, she argues, to their thorough-going differentiation between analytical constructs and the idiom employed by informants themselves (cf. Mitchell 1974). The ethnographer's role is then clearly recognized to be one of principled abstraction as distinct from unstructured and undisciplined immersion in the life-world of a group of subjects.

The analytical separation of 'insiders' and 'outsiders' accounts inevitably pushes the discussion of ethnography as method beyond a purely technical appraisal (cf. Burgess 1982; Ellen 1984). It raises issues concerning the ethnographer's ethical judgements and moral responsibilities towards his or her subjects (cf. Mitchell and Draper 1983; Jackson and Smith 1984). These questions are all the more pressing because, with few exceptions (e.g. Seeley et al. 1956; Gans 1967), the subjects of ethnographic research have tended to be the poor and relatively powerless residents of multiethnic inner-city areas. While such an emphasis has frequently been justified on the grounds of providing a sympathetic interpretation of apparently alien lifestyles and 'foreign' cultures, this liberal interpretation of the social scientist's role is now increasingly under attack. The inadvertent role of the academic in perpetuating the ideologies which contribute to the oppression of minority groups has now been repeatedly demonstrated (e.g. Bourne and Sivanandan 1980; Lawrence 1982) such that ethnographers can no longer hide behind the shield of their benign intentions.

Throughout the history of urban ethnography, too little attention has been paid to methodology. While the Chicago monographs generally neglected any specific discussion of method, some evidence of their characteristic procedures can be gleaned from the texts themselves and from such circumstantial evidence as now exists. For example, an autobiographical account of the methodology adopted by Paul Cressey has only recently been published (Bulmer 1983) providing a belated opportunity for critical evaluation of the methods employed by one of the pioneers of urban ethnography.

In general, it must be said that by present-day standards the Chicago sociologists were lax in citing the sources of their evidence and in detailing the methods of their analyses. Nevertheless, the principal criticisms which were directed at their work continue to surface today and have not been allayed by the contemporary ethnographer's greater willingness to be explicit about their methods. One of the most persistent criticisms of urban ethnography is that valid generalizations cannot be made on the basis of a single case study. Some writers will admit that ethnographic research succeeds in increasing the depth and subtlety of understanding in particular cases, but they too find the question of representativeness an insurmountable problem. Such is the tenacity of these doubts that even confirmed adherents of the ethnographic method sometimes fall prey to them. Thus, Gerald Suttles has argued that his ethnography of the 'Addams' area in Chicago 'gains in validity what it lacks in representativeness' (Suttles 1968: 12). And even Herbert Gans seeks to validate his findings in *The urban villagers* in terms of the representativeness of the West Enders whom he studied. As he argues in the updated second edition of that classic work: '*The urban villagers* was a case study and the validity of its findings depended to some extent on how representative the West Enders were of the country's Italian-Americans' (Gans 1982: 411).

On the contrary, the validity of Gans's particular findings is actually quite independent of his respondents' representativeness of the larger ethnic group. For representativeness is not the only acceptable, or indeed the most appropriate, criterion for judging the validity of case material. The positivist criteria of statistical inference have come to dominate social science to such a degree that alternative bases of validity are rarely even considered. But, as Clyde Mitchell has recently argued, making inferences from case material is in fact based on the validity of the analysis rather than on the representativeness of events (Mitchell 1983: 190).

The criterion of validity most appropriate to the case study method (and to the analysis of what Mitchell calls 'situation analysis' in general) concerns the *logical* relationship between characteristics rather than their representativeness or typicality. The logicality of this connection is in turn to be judged from the adequacy with which the wider social context is specified. The extent to which generalization may be made from case studies depends upon the adequacy of the underlying theory and the whole corpus of related knowledge of which the case forms a part rather than on the particular instance itself (Mitchell 1983: 203). What makes *The social order of the slum* (Suttles 1968) such a classic ethnography, for example, is not simply its 'perfection of the techniques of participant observation in a field setting' (Janowitz 1968), but also its routine recourse to sociological principle which gives the recorded material its analytical strength.

A related problem concerns the cumulativity (or otherwise) of ethnographic research. To what extent are the findings of one study comparable with those of any other, and how confident can one be that findings that were produced in one context will hold in any other setting? In an otherwise sympathetic review of Chicago ethnography, for example, Hannerz advances the charge that their vignettes of city life evince little theoretical cumulativity (Hannerz 1980: 55). Again, however, it might be suggested that an inappropriate model is being applied to ethnographic research. Very little research in the social sciences is cumulative in a simple additive sense. But as the preceding review demonstrates, ethnography provides the possibility for evaluation and critique even if precise criteria for judging validity are not available. In this respect, urban ethnography is not significantly different from other modes of inquiry in the social sciences and humanities where critical judgement ultimately rests with the consensus of a community of scholars.

Conclusion: Ethnography in the City

There is much in the literature of urban ethnography to excite the geographer's interest and emulation. It provides a model for sensitive, first-hand descriptions of city life with a respectable intellectual tradition already familiar to the geographer. And yet ethnography remains a persistent undercurrent in social science research rather than an integral part of the mainstream. This paper has focused on some of the theoretical and methodological problems which might serve to explain this chronic marginality. Ethnography has yet to establish a firm place in urban studies precisely because it is not yet clear what is specifically 'urban' about urban ethnography. Since the early years of the 'Chicago school', ethnographic research has not been rooted in any general theory of the urban; it has been *in* the city, rather than *of* the city (cf. Hannerz 1980; Saunders 1981).

In order to realize its full potential, therefore, urban ethnography must resolve its relationship to some of the broader theoretical questions which it has so far persistently refused to address. These questions centre on the need to locate particular ethnographies in terms of their larger social and historical context, which in turn demands that they be adequately situated theoretically. Only then will it be possible for the ethnographer to describe the negotiations of everyday social interaction without neglecting the political and economic forces of structured inequality.

Notes

1   Editorial note: Peter Jackson's essay on 'Urban Ethnography' is a classic in urban anthropology. Written as early as 1985, it remained the most comprehensive introduction into the field. Peter Jackson is addressing geographers, but his explanations are relevant for all areas of urban research.

2   Thomas defined 'disorganization' as the decrease of the influence of existing social rules of behaviour upon individual members of the group. By 'definition of the situation' Thomas attempted to describe individuals and groups according to their different perspectives on social situations. These ideas are most clearly elaborated in Thomas and Znaniecki's five-volume study of *The Polish peasant in Europe and America* (1918–20) which includes a lengthy methodological introduction.

3   The influence of Simmel on Park and on the whole interactionist tradition is traced in detail in Levine (1971) and in Jackson and Smith (1984).

4   By situational accounts, Suttles refers to the conditional nature of urban existence and to the variety of cultural strategies available in any social situation. By normative accounts, he refers to more static sociological theory concerning the standards or norms to which people claim to aspire. Suttles' own preference for the situational over the normative is indicated by his argument that 'men do not just conform, but sort around among their culture and social structure in a selective and mindful way' (Suttles 1976 2).

5   For a critical discussion of this literature, see Brown (1981).

References

Anderson, Elijah. *A place on the corner*. Chicago: University of Chicago Press, 1976.

Anderson, Nels. *The hobo*. Chicago: University of Chicago Press, 1923.

Bell, Colin and Howard Newby. *Community studies*. London: George Allen and Unwin, 1971.

Bourne, Jenny and Anil Sivanandan. 'Cheerleaders and ombudsmen: the sociology of race relations in Britain.' In *Race and Class* 21, 1980: 331–52.

Brown, Kevin R. Race. 'Class and culture: towards a theorization of the 'choice/constraint' concept.' In *Social interaction and ethnic segregation,* edited by Peter Jackson and Susan J. Smith. London: Academic Press, 1981: 185–203.

Bulmer, Martin. 'The methodology of 'The taxi-dance hall': an early account of Chicago ethnography from the 1920s.' In *Urban Life* 12, 1983: 95–120.

Burgess, Jacquelin. 'News from nowhere: the press, the riots and the myth of the inner city.' In *Geography, the media and popular culture,* edited by Jacquelin Burgess and John R. Gold. London: Croom Helm, 1985.

Burgess, Robert G., ed. *Field research: a sourcebook and field manual.* London: George Allen and Unwin, 1982.

Caplow, Theodore, Howard M. Bahr, Bruce A. Chadwick, R. Hill and Margaret H. Williamson. *Middletown families: fifty years of change and continuity.* Minneapolis: University of Minnesota Press, 1982.

Castells, Manuel. 'Is there an urban sociology?' In *Urban sociology: critical essays,* edited by C. G. Pickvance. New York: St Martin's Press, 1976: 33–59.

Castells, Manuel. *The urban question.* London: Edward Arnold, 1977.

Castells, Manuel. *The city and the grassroots.* London: Edward Arnold, 1983.

Centre for Contemporary Cultural Studies. *The empire strikes back: race and racism in 70s Britain.* London: Hutchinson, 1982.

Clarke, John, Charles Critcher and Richard Johnson, eds. *Working class culture: studies in history and theory.* London: Hutchinson, 1979.

Cloward, Richard A. and Lloyd E. Ohlin. *Delinquency and opportunity: a theory of delinquent gangs.* Glencoe, Illinois: Free Press, 1960.

Cohen, Abner. 'Drama and politics in the development of a London carnival.' In *Man* 15, 1980: 65–87.

Cohen, Abner. 'A polyethnic London carnival as a contested cultural performance.' In *Ethnic and Racial Studies* 5, 1982: 23–41.

Cohen, Albert K. *Delinquent boys: the culture of the gang.* Glencoe, Illinois: Free Press,1955.

Cressey, Paul G. *The taxi-dance hall.* Chicago: University of Chicago Press, 1932.

Drake, St. Clair and Horace R. Cayton. *Black metropolis: a study of Negro life in a Northern City.* New York: Harper and Row (second edition, 1962), 1945.

Ellen, Roy, ed. *Ethnographic research: a guide to general conduct.* London: Academic Press, 1984.

Entrikin, J. Nicholas. 'Robert Park's human ecology and human geography.' In *Annals of the Association of American Geographers* 70, 1980: 43–58.

Faris, Robert E. L. *Chicago sociology 1920–32.* San Francisco: Chandler, 1967 (Reprinted 1970, Chicago: University of Chicago Press).

Gans, Herbert J. *The Levittowners.* New York: Pantheon, 1967.

Gans, Herbert J. *The urban villagers,* second edition. New York: Free Press, 1982.

Giddens, Anthony. *Central problems in social theory.* London: Hutchinson, 1979.

Gregory, Derek. 'Human agency and human geography.' In *Transactions of the Institute of British Geographers New Series* 6, 1981: 1-18.

Hall, Stuart and Tony Jefferson, eds. *Resistance through rituals: youth subcultures in postwar Britain.* London: Hutchinson, 1976.

Hammersley, Martyn and Paul Atkinson. *Ethnography: principles in practice.* London and New York: Tavistock, 1983.

Hannerz, Ulf. *Soulside: inquiries into ghetto culture and community.* New York: Columbia University Press, 1969.

Hannerz, Ulf. *Exploring the city: inquiries towards an urban anthropology.* New York: Columbia University Press, 1980.

Harris, Richard. 'Residential segregation and class formation in the capitalist city: a review and directions for research.' In *Progress in Human Geography* 8, 1984: 26–49.

Harvey, David. *Social justice and the city.* London: Edward Arnold, 1973.

Hayner, Norman S. *Hotel life.* Chapel Hill, North Carolina: University of North Carolina Press, 1936.

Hunter, Albert. 'The Gold Coast and the slum revisited: paradoxes in replication research and the study of social change.' In *Urban Life* 11, 1983: 461–76.

Jackson, Peter. 'Principles and problems of participant observation.' In *Geografiska Annaler* 65B, 1983a: 39–46.

Jackson, Peter. 'Social geography: convergence and compromise.' In *Progress in Human Geography* 7, 1983b: 116–21.

Jackson, Peter. 'Social disorganization and moral order in the city.' In *Transactions of the Institute of British Geographers New Series* 9, 1984: 168–80.

Jackson, Peter and Susan J. Smith. 'Introduction.' In *Social interaction and ethnic segregation*, edited by Peter Jackson and Susan Smith. London: Academic Press, 1981: 1–17.

Jackson, Peter and Susan J. Smith. *Exploring social geography*. London: George Allen and Unwin, 1984.

James, William. 'On a certain blindness in human beings.' In *Talks to teachers on psychology*, edited by William James. New York: Henry Holt, 1899: 229–64.

Janowitz, Morris. 'Introduction.' In *W. I. Thomas on social organization and social personality*. Chicago: University of Chicago Press, 1966: vii–lviii.

Janowitz, Morris. 'Preface.' In *The social order of the slum,* by Gerald D. Suttles. Chicago: University of Chicago Press,1968: vii–ix.

Janowitz, Morris. *The last half-century: societal change and politics in America*. Chicago: University of Chicago Press, 1978.

Katznelson, Ira. *City trenches: urban politics and the patterning of class in the United States*. Chicago: University of Chicago Press, 1981.

Kornblum, William. *Blue collar community*. Chicago: University of Chicago Press, 1974.

Lawrence, Errol. 'In the abundance of water the fool is thirsty: sociology and black 'pathology.' In *Centre for Contemporary Cultural Studies*, 1982: 47–94.

Levine, Donald N., ed. 'Introduction.' In *Georg Simmel on individuality and social forms*. Chicago: University of Chicago Press, 1971: ix–lxv.

Levine, Donald N. 'Simmel at a distance: on the history and systematics of the sociology of the stranger.' In *Strangers in African societies,* edited by W. A. Shack and E. P. Skinner. Berkeley, California: University of California Press, 1979: 21–36.

Ley, David. *The black inner city as frontier outpost: images and behavior in a Philadelphia neighborhood*. Washington DC: Association of American Geographers, Monograph No. 7, 1974.

Ley, David. *Geography without man: a humanistic critique*. Oxford School of Geography, Research Paper No. 24, 1980.

Ley, David and Cybriwsky, Roman A. 'Urban graffiti as territorial markers.' In *Annals of the Association of American Geographers* 64, 1974: 491–505.

Liebow, Elliott. *Tally's corner: a study of Negro streetcorner men*. Boston: Little, Brown, 1967.

Lynd, Robert S. and Helen M. Lynd. *Middletown*. New York: Harcourt Brace, 1929.

Lynd, Robert S. and Helen M. Lynd. *Middletown in transition*. New York: Harcourt Brace, 1937.

Madge, John. *The origins of scientific sociology*. New York: Free Press, 1962.

Marcuse, Peter. 'The targeted crisis: on the ideology of the urban fiscal crisis and its uses.' In *International Journal of Urban and Regional Research* 5, 1981: 330–55.

Mayer, Harold M. and Richard C. Wade. *Chicago: growth of a metropolis*. Chicago: University of Chicago Press, 1969.

Mead, George H. *Mind, self and society*. Chicago: University of Chicago Press, 1934.

Mitchell, Bruce and Dianne Draper. *Relevance and ethics in geography*. London: Longman, 1982.

Mitchell, J. Clyde. 'Perceptions of ethnicity and ethnic behaviour: an empirical exploration.' In *Urban ethnicity*, edited by Abner Cohen. London: Tavistock, 1974: 1–35.

Mitchell, J. Clyde. 'Case and situation analysis.' In *Sociological Review* 31, 1983: 187–211.

Osofsky, Gilbert. *Harlem: the making of a ghetto 1890–1930,* second edition. New York: Harper Torchbooks, 1963.

Park, Robert E. 'The city as a social laboratory.' Reprinted in *Human communities: the collected writings of Robert E. Park.* Vol. II, edited by Everett C. Hughes. Glencoe, Illinois: Free Press, 1929: 73–87.

Park, Robert E. 'News as a form of knowledge.' Reprinted in *Society: the collected writings of Robert E. Park.* Vol. III, Glencoe, Illinois: Free Press, 1940: 71–88.

Park, Robert E. 'An autobiographical note.' Reprinted in *Race and culture: the collected writings of Robert E. Park.* Vol. I, edited by Everett C. Hughes. Glencoe, Illinois: Free Press, 1950: v–ix.

Park, Robert E. *Human communities: the collected writings of Robert E. Park.* Vol. II, edited by Everett C. Hughes. Glencoe, Illinois: Free Press, 1952.

Park, Robert E. and Ernest W. Burgess, eds. *The city.* Chicago: University of Chicago Press (1967 edition), 1925.

Peach, Ceri. 'Introduction: the spatial analysis of ethnicity and class.' In *Urban social segregation*, edited by Ceri Peach. London: Longman, 1975: 1–17.

Polsky, Ned. *Community power and political theory.* New Haven, Connecticut: Yale University Press, 1963.

Rock, Paul. *The making of symbolic interactionism.* London: Macmillan, 1979.

Saunders, Peter. *Social theory and the urban question.* London: Hutchinson, 1981.

Seeley, John R., R. Alexander Sim and Elizabeth W. Loosley. *Crestwood Heights.* New York: Basic Books, 1956.

Short, James F. Jr. 'Introduction.' In *The gang,* by Frederic M. Thrasher. Chicago: University of Chicago Press (abridged edition), 1963: xv–liii.

Simmel, Georg. 'The metropolis and mental life,' 1903. Reprinted in *Georg Simmel on individuality and social forms*, edited by Donald N. Levine. Chicago: University of Chicago Press, 1971: 324–39.

Simmel, Georg. 'The stranger,' 1908. Reprinted in *Georg Simmel on individuality and social forms*, edited by D. N. Levine. Chicago: University of Chicago Press, 1971: 143-49.

Simmel, Georg. *Conflict and the web of group affiliations.* New York: Free Press, 1955.

Smith, Susan J. 'Humanistic method in contemporary social geography.' In *Area* 13, 1981: 293–98.

Smith, Susan J. 'Practicing humanistic geography.' In *Annals of the Association of American Geographers* 74, 1984a: 353–74.

Smith, Susan J. 'Negotiating ethnicity in an uncertain environment.' In *Ethnic and Racial Studies* 7, 1984b: 360–73.

Snodgrass, Jon, ed. *The jack-roller at seventy: a fifty-year follow up.* Lexington, Massachusetts: D. C. Heath, 1982.

Spear, Allan H. *Black Chicago. The making of a Negro ghetto 1890–1920.* Chicago: University of Chicago Press, 1967.

Stein, Maurice R. *The eclipse of community*, second edition. New York: Harper Torchbooks, 1964.

Steinberg, Stephen. *The ethnic myth.* Boston, Massachusetts: Beacon Press, 1981.

Stonequist, Everett. *The marginal man.* New York: Scribner's, 1937.

Susser, Ida. *Norman Street: poverty and politics in an urban neighborhood.* New York: Oxford University Press, 1982.

Suttles, Gerald D. *The social order of the slum.* Chicago: University of Chicago Press, 1968.

Suttles, Gerald D. 'Urban ethnography: situational and normative accounts.' In *Annual Review of Sociology* 2, 1976: 1–18.

Thomas, William I. and Florian Znaniecki. *The Polish peasant in Europe and America*, 5 vols. Boston, Massachusetts: Richard G. Badger, 1918–20.

Thrasher, Frederic M. *The gang,* 1927. Chicago: University of Chicago Press (1967 edition).

Turner, Ralph H. 'Introduction.' In *Robert E. Park on social control and collective behavior*. Chicago: University of Chicago Press, 1967: ix–xlvi.

Wallman, Sandra. *Eight London households*. London: Tavistock, 1984.

Ward, David. 'The ethnic ghetto in the United States: past and present.' In *Transactions of the Institute of British Geographers New Series* 7, 1982: 257–75.

Warner, W. Lloyd. *Yankee City*. New Haven, Connecticut: Yale University Press (abridged edition), 1963.

Warner, W. Lloyd and Josiah O. Low. *The social system of a modern factory*. New Haven, Connecticut: Yale University Press, 1947.

Whyte, William F. *Street corner society,* second edition. Chicago: University of Chicago Press, 1955.

Wirth, Louis. 'A bibliography of the urban community.' In *The city,* edited by Robert E. Park and Ernest W. Burgess, 1925: 161–228.

Wirth, Louis. *The ghetto*. Chicago: University of Chicago Press, 1928.

NELE BRÖNNER WITH LES BACK

Les Back

Inscriptions of Love

The routes of a life spent in transit are inscribed on his skin. At rest now, he lies motionless, voiceless, in a hospital bed. The nurse interprets the 'vital signs' transmitted from his body. An internal struggle is encoded in these readings like a Morse code message from a vessel in peril at sea. There is no external trace of the great effort going on inside him and the elderly man cannot speak of what brought him to this point. As he lies there, his body represents an illustrated map of his life.

The tattoos that covered his arms and chest each bore the name of a place: Burma, Singapore and Malaysia. Each of them had a record of the year the inscription was made. He had been a merchant seaman and had travelled the world. On his right arm was the figure of an Indian woman dancing with her hands clasped together above her head, her skin darkened by the tattooist's ink. In the sailor's autumn years the figure etched on this pale canvas had turned a deep shade of blue. On the left forearm was an inscription that marked his journey's end: a tattoo of Tower Bridge, London and beneath it the dedication – 'HOME'. It read like an anchor.[1]

The voiceless patient spoke beyond sound. These tattoos told a story of the places he had visited, the voyages in between, and contained allusions to intimacies shared in tattoo parlours around the world. Here the sailor trusted local artists enough – in India and Burma – to spill blood and mark his flesh indelibly. On the surfaces of this failing body was a history of the relationship between the sailor's metropolitan home and the hinterlands of trade and empire. The permeability of that relationship – between imperial centre and colonial periphery – was marked on the porous membranes of his dying body.

The most familiar account of the history of the tattoo in Britain and the West is that this practice was brought back to Europe in the eighteenth century when European explorers encountered the tattooing cultures of the South Pacific and Polynesia. Captain James Cook's voyages gave the English language the word tattoo. He observed the practice on Tahiti in July 1769.[2] It is a variation of a Polynesian term *tatu* or *tatau* meaning to mark or strike.[3] On Cook's second circumnavigation of the globe he transported Omai to London. This man, from Raiatea Island close to Tahiti, became an exotic curiosity in London, in part because he bore the marks of Polynesian tattooing that Cook had described earlier.[4] Cook's ships and the 'specimen' contained within them were unloaded on the south bank of the river Thames just a few miles away from where the sailor whose description opened this chapter lay in his hospital bed.

The emphasis placed on the encounter with Polynesian tattooing cultures has occluded histories of earlier bodily inscription in Britain and Europe. In particular, various historians have shown the connection between tattooing and penal and property rights among the Greeks, Romans and Celts.[5] Also, early Christians in Roman territories inscribed their bodies as an expression of the devotee's servitude to Christ.[6] More than this, there is a connection between pilgrimage and tattooing. Early modern pilgrims to Palestine were tattooed with Christian symbols available in Jerusalem and brought their marked bodies home as evidence of their sacred travels. This practice also occurred among pilgrims to the Shrine of Loreto in Italy in the sixteenth century. There is then a strong connection between travel and tattooing.

Alfred Gell has concluded that the stigma associated with tattooing in the West results from a double association of the 'ethnic Other' and the 'class Other'.[7] Tattooing was drawn into the culture and vernacular of the sailors themselves and the cultural world they created. Historian Marcus Rediker has shown that a life on the sea left its mark on the bodies of working-class seamen.

> The tattoo, then and now, often adorned his forearm. 'The Jerusalem Cross' and other popular designs were made by 'pricking the skin, and rubbing in a pigment', either ink, or, more often gunpowder. Seafaring left other, unwanted distinguishing marks. Prolonged exposure to the sun and its intensified reflection off the water gave him a tanned or reddened – 'metal coloured' – and prematurely wrinkled look … thus in many ways the seaman was a marked man, much to the delight of the press gangs that combed the port towns in search of seamen to serve the crown.[8]

Rediker identifies a key paradox. In working-class life, tattooing has provided a way of reclaiming and aestheticizing the body. At the same time these marks sketch the outline of a 'class Other', a target for respectable society to recognize and stigmatize, be it in the form of a press gang, officers of the law, or today's bourgeois moralists.

The painted sailor is gone now; his life has ebbed away. His passing was noted by the registrar of the void who recorded his lapsed life and issued a flimsy certificate. The inscription of his body was an attempt to make an enduring mark, yet he belonged to a class of people for whom there is little place in the official record. 'They are the sort of people', noted Patrick Modiano, 'who leave few traces'.[9] Gruesome exceptions are held in the specimen laboratory at Guy's Hospital, London. Here, pieces of marked skin are preserved in the acrid smelling jars of formalin. The peeled skins are the only traces of nameless men from whose arms they were taken. They show the images of a Hope and Anchor and of Christ crucified, grafts that were taken, or filched, for medical research.[10] This is still happening, although in today's National Health Service 'progress' demands some payment upfront. Jock Browning, for example, out of Waterloo, London has left his almost completely tattooed body 'to science'. In return he received the meagre sum of £ 3,000.[11]

Having a tattoo, or being pierced, is a moment when boundaries are breached, involving hurt and healing. It is profoundly a corporeal experience – the piercing of the skin, the flow of blood, pain, the forming of a scab, the healing of the wound and the visible trace of this process of incision and closure. It involves perforating the boundary between the internal and external so that the external becomes internal and the internal becomes external. The tattoo itself can be read through a range of metaphors, for example, the relationships between agency and control, permanence and ephemerality, trauma and healing. Such associations are never straightforward and rarely just a matter of individual choice. As Alfred Gell pointed out: 'The apparently selfwilled tattoo always turns out to have been elicited by others.'[12]

The Body as a Political Field

Michel Foucault is perhaps the most eloquent analyst of the ways in which the body acts as a site of cultural and political manipulation. He writes in *Discipline and Punish*: 'The body is also directly involved in a political field; power relations have an immediate hold upon it; they invest it, mark it, train it, torture it, force it to carry out tasks, to perform ceremonies, to emit signs.'[13] Elsewhere he concludes that 'the body is the surface of the inscription of events'.[14] For Foucault, this is both a process whereby the 'Me' of identity is constituted by history and power, but also a site of perpetual disintegration. In his sense the body is 'totally imprinted by history'.[15]

Franz Kafka provides a chilling illustration of a Foucauldian sense of discipline through inscription in his short story 'In the Penal Colony'. In the story, the law of the prison is enforced through a novel tattooing machine composed of a bed, with cotton wool, and, above the bed, held in place with metal rods, a Designer. Each machine resembles a dark wooden chest. Between the Designer and the Bed shuttles a skin-writing device on a ribbon of steel called the Harrow. The Officer of the Colony explains this method of punishment: 'Whatever commandment the prisoner has disobeyed is written upon his body by the Harrow. 'This prisoner for instance' – the officer indicated the man – 'will have written on his body: HONOUR THY SUPERIORS!'[16] Prisoners are not informed of their sentence. The Officer in the story explains why: 'There would be no point in telling him. He'll learn it on his body.'[17] This chilling tale is not so far from the truth of the ways in which tattooing has been used as a tool for punishment. Think of the numbers tattooed on the Jewish and other prisoners of the Nazi concentration camps. Here the tattoo was a means of regulation, control and initiation into the world of the camp. In the aftermath of liberation, the survivors have had to carry with them these marks as a permanent reminder. Primo Levi documents his return from Auschwitz in his extraordinary book *The Truce,* writing, as he passed through Germany, 'I felt the tattooed number on my arm burning like a sore.'[18]

Tattooing continues today inside prisons, but now it is the prisoners who tattoo themselves. Susan Phillips illustrates this point in her brilliant study of gangland tattooing:

> No longer tattooed or branded by those who incarcerate them, prisoners now mark themselves forever into the stigmatised world of the prison. Tattooing creates permanent representations of identity that cannot be taken away by the authorities; they represent positive affirmations of self in an environment full of negatives. Even if the prisoners are stripped of clothes, have their heads shaven, are forced into tiny cells, are bloodied by each other or prison guards, tattoos speak of their pasts and carry the strength of their affiliations.[19]

Tattooing, prohibited in US prisons, has become a means to wrest control over the prisoner's body from the grey concrete institutions. Phillips tells the story of one tattoo artist called Gallo. He was in prison for eight years and during this time he earned money as a tattooist. Caught by the guards, he consequently had to serve an extra six months. Gallo's body was marked with gangland tattoos, through which he visibly brought his neighbourhood affiliations into the prison. As a result he received protection and support. Outside, his tattoos and his physical appearance had a paradoxical allure. On the one hand, it meant that he was offered parts in hard-core pornography films: for pornographic film-makers, tattooed gang members apparently provide a means to titillate the viewer with images of dangerous exoticism. But, at the same time, his tattoos also marked Gallo out as a target for the police. Phillips lost contact with him, when Gallo was on the verge of another prison sentence after being arrested again for possession of soft drugs.[20] So Gallo's tattoos are about both affirmation and damnation, arousing both desire and disgust.

There are connections between Gallo's experience and tattooing in the United Kingdom. In media representations images of tattooed men are associated with violence and football hooliganism. Similarly, tattooed working-class women have been associated, up until quite recently, with sexual deviance, prostitution and criminality. A press report described a working-class community in southern England as a place of 'cigarettes, hamburgers and tattoos'.[21] All of these attributes were connected in one form or another with abuses of the body. In 2004 the term Chav became the new shorthand to describe the disreputable members of the white working class. For young women the signs of Chav style include wearing large gold loop earrings, flashy 'bling' jewellery and clothing brands such as Burberry, Adidas, Nike and Timberland, and having their hair tied back in a tight pony tail dubbed the 'Croydon face lift'.[22] Julie Burchill refers to the class stereotypes as a form of 'social racism'.[23] Others have luxuriated in the anti-charisma charisma of Chavism, resulting in websites that proudly extol its virtues, vices, cultural habits and hallmarks.[24]

The etymology of the term 'Chav' is contested. Some suggest that it is a distortion of the Anglo-Romani word 'charvi', meaning child, while others claim it is derived from 'Chatham girls'. Most agree that Cheltenham, Gloucestershire provided its origin: here local working-class youths were referred to as 'Cheltenham Averages' by the disapproving middle-class students and parents at Cheltenham Ladies' College, and the phrase was subsequently shortened to 'Chavs'. In the venomous popular book *Chav! A User's Guide to Britain's New Ruling Class* the display of tattoos is described as a means for Chavs to announce summer's arrival: 'Most of these will usually feature the name of most recent partner, offspring or dead grandparent. Working on the "waste not, want not" principle, the more resourceful of the species will always try to cover up last year's partner's name with this year's – which usually results in an even more elaborate design feature.'[25] The chav phenomenon has reinvigorated a class prejudice that is primarily and tellingly defined through body culture and style.

These are just recent manifestations of long-standing class-inflected forms of stigma. Part of what I want to do in what follows is look closely at classinflected forms of embodiment and emotional life, kinship and love. More than this, I want to use this impulse to raise a series of questions about the relationship between the body, language and memory. How does the body become a medium and a fleshy canvas through and on which belonging and structures of feeling are expressed? In what sense does the reliance on elaborated forms of language obscure the modes of expression held within white working-class contexts with regard to emotional life, attachment, love and loss? It is not only that 'the nameless' live and die without trace, but also that the complexity of their emotional lives is lost, ignored or disparaged.

So the project that is contained here is a reckoning with memory, culture and history, particularly of the white working-class communities that traverse inner and outer London south of the river. It is an attempt to approach the biography of 'the nameless' through the medium of the tattoo. Photographer Paul Halliday and I have worked closely together on the portraits that form the basis of this chapter. We worked jointly in the production of these images. We approached people who, for one reason or another, had decided to have tattoos inscribed. The participants were all familiar to us, some were friends and others family members. From the outset we wanted this project to be about an exchange that was both palpable – of giving photographs once they were made – but also a dialogue of sentiments and recollections that were shown as well as written. It is in the showing that the largest part of the story is told.

Speaking and Showing

An implicit impulse in some strains of radical sociology – particularly those inspired by the political projects of feminism and anti-racism – is the desire and expectation that the disenfranchised should speak for themselves. This is a compelling challenge for sociology, but ultimately it is a deceptive hope. The idea itself presupposes the form of interaction in which the voice is rendered. The sociological interview, for example, privileges the idioms of elaborated communication, so often infused with class bias. As the late Basil Bernstein pointed out, class divisions are echoed in language use. On occasions where faithfully, and idiomatically, transcribed working-class speech makes it onto the page, it jars the eye. The results can read like a Dick Van Dyke caricature of chirpy Cockney brogue. Bernstein argued that restricted language codes among working-class people result in distinctions that are tattooed metaphorically on their tongues.[26] Within this context working-class people articulate themselves through other means.

The prophetic philosopher Simone Weil once commented that 'affliction' – a notion that she held to be both material and spiritual – is by its nature inarticulate. She writes:

> the afflicted are not listened to. They are like someone whose tongue has been cut out and who occasionally forgets the fact. When they move their lips no ear perceives any sound. And they themselves soon sink into impotence in the use of language, because of the certainty of not being heard. That is why there is no hope for the vagrant as he stands before the magistrate. Even if, through his stammerings, he should utter a cry to pierce the soul, neither the magistrate nor the public will hear it. His cry is mute.[27]

In order to avoid replicating the plight of the magistrate, we need to recognize that people express themselves through a wider range of cultural modalities that operate beyond the word. Zygmunt Bauman concluded: 'Is it not so that when everything is said about matters most important to human life, the most important things remain unsaid?'[28]

Paul and I have tried to use photography to access the registers of embodied forms of communication. Much has been written about the way the photographic lens operates to survey and govern the definition of what is 'real'.[29] But it is a mistake, I think, to see the lens as only looking one way. This raises the question posed by John Berger, namely 'Who is looking at Who?'[30] An answer is provided in the philosophical writings of Maurice Merleau-Ponty, who argues against the legacy of

Cartesian dualism that separates mind from body, subject from object. He makes a case for the importance of developing a sensuous understanding and stresses that 'we are in the world through our body'.[31] Instead of dividing between subject and object, he stresses an intertwining, or a chiasm. For him 'the look' doesn't produce distance, a gap between the viewer and the looked upon. Rather, the look produces a connection. It involves openness to being that is potentially two-way or 'reversible' in Merleau-Ponty's language. 'It is the coiling of the visible upon the seeing body', he writes. 'I lend them my body in order that they inscribe upon it and give me their resemblance, this fold, this central cavity of the visible which is my vision, these two mirror arrangements of the seeing and the visible, the touching and the touched...'[32] This process of intertwining occurs at the moment when the seer and the visible connect. It is made on the stage of everyday life but it also possesses a specific relationship to time. In that fraction of a second when the aperture of the camera opens, a tiny slice of time is preserved in which the relationship between the viewer and the looked upon is caught, and held, in place.

The Lion's Face

Mick looks back at us from the other side of the lens (Figure 1). Through his look he addresses us but we have to listen with our eyes as well as our ears. He was born in Lewisham in 1951 and lived as a child in Perry Vale, Forest Hill, South London. Mick shows the two lions inscribed on his chest. They are the totem of his football team, Millwall Football Club, known to friend and foe alike as 'The Lions'. In the public imagination, Millwall signifies everything that is deplorable in English football culture – violence, bigotry and hatred. In his fascinating study of the club and its history, Garry Robson writes:

> The word Millwall, I would suggest, is one of the most evocative in contemporary English. It functions as a condensed symbol, widely and indiscriminately used to express ideas and feelings about an entire sphere of activity and experience well beyond the compass of its original meaning. It has become a byword for, amongst other things, violent mob thuggery, unreconstructed masculinity, dark and impenetrable urban culture and working class 'fascism'.[33]

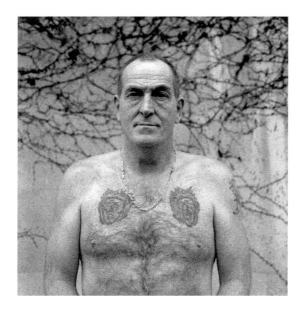

This caricature holds little resemblance for the devoted fans for which the club provides a sense of belonging and affiliation, passion and love. For within this 'condensed symbol' are the vestiges of an urban history that is largely ignored by journalists and politicians who are quick to condemn Millwall's fans as proto-fascist football hooligans. Mick's grandmother was from Donegal in Ireland and his aunts live in various parts of Ireland. He started following Millwall when he was nine years old. He speaks of the fun and intoxicating atmosphere of football culture of that time:

> The best times – going to watch Millwall play away was special because the excitement, the adrenaline was there from the Friday evening. Going in the old pubs and having a drink, you know, don't matter what age it was … we always sneaked you in or they sneaked me in or whatever, but no it was … it was, the adrenaline was there on a Friday evening, or especially if you was travelling on a Friday evening because in them days you had no motorways and you went overnight,

places like Carlisle and Barrow and Workington ... We went up over-
night and it was, it was you know, just brilliant, you know, just travel-
ling and letting other people see that you're. You're there like, and
you've come all this way like to see Millwall play and then ... the, the
high point was at the end of the game, you know ... If we'd won like,
you know what I mean, you was over the moon like, you know. Or
very disappointed if you lose because the long dreary drive back like,
you know ... Well as I say, we've had some brilliant times.[34]

Mick was filmed for a notorious television documentary made by the *Panorama* team
in the early 1970s. The programme was an exposé of football hooliganism focusing
on Millwall. As a result, Mick's face was plastered up unfairly in football grounds
with 'mug shots' of the most wanted 'Millwall hooligans'. The Millwall fraternity
was populated by legendary figures like Ginger Bob, Ray Treatment, Harry The
Dog, Tiny – who was a black Millwall fan and one of the most respected – and Sid
the 'Umbrella Man'. Mick explained:

Well, we used to go to football matches and when the trouble was on
Sid just walked, [he] always had an umbrella with him and as though
he weren't causing no trouble. Then when you get the supporters running by like, the opposition he'd chchsh [pull them around the neck],
that with the umbrella like and chhh – it was comical. I mean we know
it was wrong but in them days it was comical because you was there,
you was a part of it.[35]

This world constituted a public sphere of life for these men between home and
work, a place that was controlled by them, enjoyed by them, and which possessed
unique emotion and electricity.

Mick had the lions inscribed on his chest when he was seventeen in Ringo's tattoo parlour in Woolwich. It was the ultimate gesture of commitment. 'I think it just
got it in your blood – obviously in them days you were tattooed up and you had sort
of lions put on you, and like Millwall Forever.'[36]

Mick collects statues of lions which decorate his home. At one point he even
owned a tame lion called Sheba, which he kept in Bexleyheath, and brought it on
several match days to The Den, Millwall's ground. These affinities are about much

Figure 2: Darren's Millwall lion
(© by Paul Halliday)

more than a sporting pastime. It is about a sense of place and of being in the world. It is a form of identification that is acted out, performed and felt both in and through the body. It is something that Mick and others like him struggle to put into words:

> I've … been supporting Millwall and um – I don't know, I think it's just territory … just, they own it, it's Millwall and that's it, and it's, and it stays, [coughs], as I say that, that, that's what it is about Millwall, it's just – Millwall is … it's they're in lights, Les, do you know what I mean, it's, it's there, it's there in lights, I mean everybody sees Millwall, everybody sees Millwall, everybody dreams Millwall.[37]

Ultimately, words are not necessary. This passion and commitment is shown. Yet, Mick didn't want the word 'Millwall' as part of his tattoo. For him the lions carry a symbolic weight that makes the affiliation to Millwall and south London clear, while remaining partially hidden from the disapproving eyes of the uninitiated.

At the time when this photograph was taken Darren was a porter at Goldsmiths College (see Figure 2). Like Mick, he grew up in south London and is a lifelong

Millwall fan. Like many he has moved out of the capital, in large part as a response to the inflation in house prices. He lived with his family in Walderslade, Kent. He commuted to his job in New Cross, a return trip of seventy miles a day. Inscribed on Darren's forearm is the fighting lion, above which is the club's name and beneath it the club's initials. This is the most beloved of all Millwall symbols. It was the club's trademark emblem up until 1999 when the club decided to ditch it in an attempt to distance itself from associations within the media with violence and hooliganism. This hasn't dented the popularity of this sign in the tattoo parlours of south London. Darren wears the tattoo proudly on his forearm alongside others that draw on styles currently sweeping Europe and America as part of what has been referred to the 'tattoo renaissance'.[38] The two styles sit together, or they seemed to when this photograph was taken in 2001. Looking at it five years later, it is possible that the angular block tattoo that separated the lion from the unicorn is a 'cover up' and the blocks of ink hide an earlier inscription.

Football tattoos attest to the wearer's commitment to their club but are also a mark of rootedness in a particular place. Many have talked about the ways in which football grounds become sacred turf.[39] Some football fans take this 'geopiety'[40] literally – they ask to be married on the pitch, or request that upon their death their ashes should be scattered in the goalmouth. Many a nighttime guerrilla raid has been performed on stadiums in south London and elsewhere to honour promises – often illegally – and administer unofficial funeral rites. Tattoos work in the opposite direction. What they do is incarnate a sense of place, community and history on the skin of the individual. Steve Scholes, a 34-year-old Manchester United fanatic, has had the entire Old Trafford Stadium tattooed on his back. The portraits show an aerial view of the ground in detail along with the words 'Old Trafford Theatre of Dreams' . He told *The Sun* newspaper, 'I just hope they don't do any more building work.'[41] This sense of place with all its associated affiliations is deposited on the body like a bearing from which orientations to life are taken as the person moves physically through different localities and over time.

It is not just that collective loyalties are written on the body through the tattoo. One of the characteristics of working-class tattoos is that names of family members and lovers are often written on the skin. This is particular to working-class tattooing. Rarely in the contemporary 'modern primitive' European tattooing subcultures – which are largely middle class – are family names inscribed.[43] There is something telling in this, which points to the class-specific nature of such practices.

In white working-class culture, the tattooed names are often the embodiment of filial love and kinship.

In her book *All About Love* bell hooks writes that 'The men in my life have always been the folks who are wary of using the word "love" lightly ... They are wary because they believe women make too much of love.'[43] In this much-needed book, hooks concluded that the lack of clarity over the meaning of love lay at the heart of the difficulty of loving. Love for her is a matter of will, action and choice. It is a matter of education. 'To truly love we must learn to mix various ingredients – care, affection, recognition, respect, commitment and trust as well as honest open communication.'[44] But what mode of communication is being insinuated here? Much has been made of the emotional inarticulacy of men in general and working-class men in particular. Gary Oldman's film *Nil By Mouth* is, in my view, the best and most intense expression of this.[45] In the film the main protagonist describes his father's internment in a hospital. Above his bed are the words 'Nil By Mouth'. This sums up the son's relationship to his father.

Speaking casually of love can debase its currency. Julie Burchill has written that there is a class dimension to the language of emotions.[46] Burchill, an acerbic and controversial journalist, has argued that middle-class families profess love quickly leading to a jejune superficiality in emotional matters. There is something in this reproach. We live in the age of the talk show exposé and reality TV where emotions have been spectacularized. Emotion talk and disclosure is now a big industry. The ratings for the 'shocking truth' television shows and the circulation of gossip magazines attest to this fact. The lack of emotional garrulousness in working-class culture points to alternative modalities in loving.

On the inside of Darren's forearm, distinct from the fierce Millwall Lion, is another tattoo (Figure 3). It consists of two names – Molly and Charley – that are linked together with a heart and beneath is a date, 26 April 1999. This marks the birthday of his beloved twin daughters. There is something beautiful and moving in the illustration of parental devotion. Love is given a name; it is incarnate. But this commitment is not made in elaborated speeches. It is performed rather than described. It is a kind of illocutionary love, a love that is expressed without painstaking announcement.

My intention here is not simply to accuse the bourgeois moralist of being blind to these complex sentiments and registers of love. The likes of Michael Collins and Julie Burchill view anti-working-class feeling as the last respectable prejudice, but

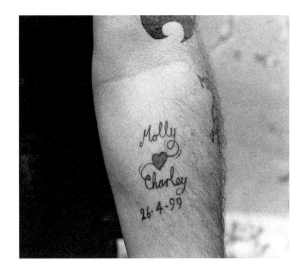

the kinds of victimology that result from this avoid serious attention being paid to the damage that class divisions inflict.[47] Romanticism and nostalgia is not simply confined to working-class boys and girls who have made good, but there is a long-standing tradition of this on the left. Working-class people are not ennobled by class inequalities, but they are often damaged by them. Part of the damage is that the powerful in the dominant order try to make working-class people in their own image, be it in terms of economic life and consumption or national affinity and belonging. It is the nature of the damage that needs attention, even if paying truth the courtesy of serious effort results at another level in the betrayal of the people we are listening to.

What remains unsaid about Darren's tattoos is what happened to him after the photographs were taken. In 2004, with Millwall's old east London rivals – West Ham – back in the same division after being relegated from the Premier League, Darren was seduced by the allure of his old ways. When West Ham visited Mill-wall's home ground, all the 'Old School' firms of football fans turned out. The police kept the fans apart and a meet had been arranged between rival 'hooligan' firms at London Bridge but it never happened. By mobile phone they arranged to meet in a pub in Stratford. Millwall turned up 'mob handed', twenty-five strong, and the pub was wrecked; a billboard was thrown through the pub window. Darren was arrested on the platform of Stratford Station.

In the run-up to the court case he began to drink heavily. He was picked up for drink driving and he lost his licence. He slipped further and further into a mood of resentment and he was pictured on a National Front rally in one of the Medway towns. His wife left him and he is separated from his twin daughters. At the time of writing, he has served the community service that resulted from his conviction for football violence and he is being treated for his alcoholism. Although he could have returned to his job at Goldsmiths College he chose not to. Of course, Darren's story is not just a parable about the injuries of class, and the contrast that Mick's story provides shows that other routes are navigated through life. The presence of racism and resentment and the double-edged nature of local patriotism and pride is at play within Darren's story, as it is more broadly within white working-class life in south-east London. It is the task of sociological listening to render this moral and political complexity without either becoming an apologist for racism or reducing such lives to a caricature of absolute evil and violent thuggery.

The Name of the Father

Michael Young was a formidable public intellectual and a keen listener to everyday life. Author of the sociological classic *Family and Kinship in East London* (with Peter Wilmott), he also founded the Open University and wrote the historic *Let Us Face the Future* 1945 manifesto for the Labour Party, which provided the blueprint for the British welfare state. When he died in 2002, his son Toby wrote a moving tribute to his father. As a young man Toby Young was exasperated with his father's antics and rebelled against his social democratic politics. One Christmas morning Michael Young disappeared to spend some time in an East End cemetery. He had heard that lonely East Enders congregated there to be with their lost loved ones, returning to the district for the day after having moved away. By the time Michael Young returned to his home, the Christmas dinner was spoilt and his family furious. Toby Young remembered: 'He waited patiently for our anger to die down and then began to tell us about the poor, grieving widows he'd seen pouring tea into the graves of their husbands so they could share one last "Christmas cuppa". Within a few minutes we'd all burst into tears.'[48]

The story caught my imagination partly because of Young's gift for sociological attention and his intuitive sense that something was at stake in the strange spectacle of women pouring tea into the graves of their lost loves. Through the Institute of Community Studies, which he founded and used as his intellectual base, now renamed the Young Foundation in his memory, I found the reference to the article he published in *The Independent* newspaper. Disappointingly, there is no description of cups of tea shared between the living and the dead. Young's ethnographic realism wouldn't allow for such a fanciful piece of trivia, rather the Newham cemetery is depicted through the conventions of modernist ethnography. He wrote:

> No one seemed to be hurrying over their work, for it was work that most of them were doing, gently removing the faded and dead flowers and leaves, brushing or even polishing the stones, planting flowers, putting the cut chrysanthemums into their holders, replacing the old artificial blooms. Where the burial was more recent they were sprucing up the Scottie dogs made of white flowers – a kind of topiary – and the wreaths shaped in the form of names: Dad or Son or Ken.[49]

The resonance of this will soon be clear, but I want to foreground Young's listening ability and his brilliant sociological intuition. Where the uninitiated would have derided the crass floral tributes and plastic graveside flower arrangements, he understood the power of the name in the emotional life of the working classes and their memory rituals. The same processes are at play, I want to suggest, in the inscriptions of love that are made through the tattooist's ink on the skin's canvas.

In her study *Formations of Class and Gender,* Beverley Skeggs demonstrates the ways in which the body and bodily dispositions carry the markers of social class. The young women in her study concentrate on their bodies as a means of self-improvement. As Julie, one of the respondents, says, 'Your body's the only thing you've got that's really yours.'[50] For these women 'letting yourself go' is surrender to the strictures of class, immobility and confinement. Another, Therese, observes: 'You know you see them walking round town, dead fat, greasy hair, smelly clothes, dirty kids, you know the type, Crimplene trousers and all, they just don't care no more, I'd never be like that.'[51] Holding onto the hollow promises of class mobility is reduced to a matter of working on a healthy diet, keeping slim and working out. Skeggs concludes, 'The working class body which is signalled through fat is the one that has given up

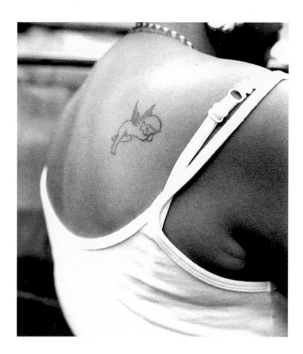

Figure 4: Vicki's angel
(© by Paul Halliday)

the hope of ever "improving".[52] Beverley Skeggs doesn't mention the place of tattooing in her discussion of the complexities of working-class femininity. But I would guess that the tattoo would have been added to the attributes connected with the ignominy of the working-class female body. Up until relatively recently, being tattooed would have engendered for young women accusations of involvement in sexual promiscuity or prostitution and being a 'slag' or 'sluttish'. The tattoo renaissance of the last ten years has changed this situation to some degree as more and more women have worn tattoos and the stigma associated with them has lessened.

On Vicki's shoulder is a tattoo of an angel (see Figure 4). She did not want her face shown. On her left shoulder, opposite this tattoo, is a 'little devil'. Her family think these sentinels of the divine and the wicked compete for influence over her personality. She is my niece and lives in New Addington, a large council estate in Croydon on the outskirts of south London and mentioned in Chapter 1. It is a place where the city and the country cut into each other like the teeth of a saw. Approximately 30,000 people live on the estate, with around 19,000 children. In 1956 Sir Hugh Casson, architectural director of the Festival of Britain, said of this estate that it was 'cut off, not only from Croydon and London, but even from life itself'.[53] Early residents called it 'Little Siberia' because it is high up on a hill and exposed to the elements. In the early 1970s Jamie Reid, who designed the artwork for the Sex Pistols, published a political magazine called *The Suburban Press* and in 1972 it ran a special edition on the politics of housing, focusing on New Addington. The editorial came to a prescient conclusion:

> New Addington has become Croydon's dumping ground for the working-class … Your only way out of an estate like Addington is to buy your way out. Work your life away for a taste of middle class life, so someone else can move in to your council house to better themselves. It is ideal for predominantly middle class Croydon to 'hide its workers away' on estates like New Addington.[54]

Jamie Reid predicted precisely what was to happen in the 1980s during the Conservative governments led by Margaret Thatcher, who offered those who could afford it the 'right to buy' with the result that the best housing stock was sold, leaving in large measure only the hard-to-let property in the public sector. Today, the skyline is dominated by the three skyscrapers that make up Canary Wharf. They resemble a giant inverted three pin-plug. Through these towers London is connected to the financial electricity of globalization. In the digital age a 'Cockney' is defined not by being born within the sound of Bow Bells, but rather within sight of Canary Wharf.

Vicki is twenty years old and at the time this photograph was taken she had just come home from her job in a supermarket. I asked her if there was any stigma involved in girls having tattoos these days. 'No', she replied. 'Everyone has got tattoos now. All kinds of things. Dolphins, things like that. They are cheap, too.' I asked her how much. 'Depends where you go, but you can get a small one done for £20–30.'[55] She showed the tattoo on her ankle (Figure 5). She was wearing her work shoes. On her ankle is a small red rose with 'Mum' and 'Dad' inked on either side of it. Illocutionary love.

Vicki shows her hands (Figure 6). Behind every piece of her gold jewellery lies a story. The third finger of her left hand warms the ring once worn by her maternal grandmother, who passed away ten years ago. Next to the gold rose, on her middle

Figure 5: Illocutionary love (© by Paul Halliday)   Figure 6: A life in her hands (© by Paul Halliday)

finger is a 'keeper ring', like the one her paternal grandfather wore, this one in fact given to her by her grandparents for her thirteenth birthday. The rings on her right hand all carry similar associations and attachments. She bought the diamond lattice ring on her index finger with the money that her maternal grandfather gave her the year that he died. The gold ring on the third finger was given to her by her paternal grandparents for her sixteenth birthday. On the middle finger of her right hand is the large gold sovereign ring given to her on her eighteenth birthday by her paternal grandmother alone. Just two months prior to Vicki's coming of age her grandfather died of cancer.

Her nails are done, professionally manicured. The extravagant artificial fingernails contain a jewel in the centre of each individual nail, a style currently popular among black and white girls in London. The phrase 'dripping in gold' is used as a means to pour scorn on working-class women. It is meant to fix young women and the nouveau riche as brash or gaudy Chavs, and mark them as inferior within the hierarchies of taste and class distinction.[56] It is a stock phrase in the lexicon of class conceit. Each of the items that Vicki wears carries a meaning and association that escapes the strictures of bourgeois ignorance and prejudice. Each symbolizes a moment passed in living, a register of love or kinship to those near to her, or to the memory of the lost. The story of her young life is in her hands.

There is a tattoo above the gold bracelet on Vicki's left wrist. It is a simple one in a contemporary style. Its presence beneath the gold jewellery signals a cultural trace from the past alive in the present. In the early period of the industrial revolution, workers had ornaments written on their skin. They had few possessions but 'free labour' meant they held sovereign power over their bodies. James Bradley concluded in his study of class and Victorian tattooing, 'Tattoos provided a substitute for jewellery, or other material possessions: a means of articulating emotion to, and forging attachments between the body, the self and others.'[17] The gold jewellery and Vicki's tattoos produce a continuity in which elements oscillate between past and present. They fit together within what Raymond Williams called a 'structure of feeling' that furnishes working-class taste and experience.[18]

Vicki's grandfather, my father, died in 1999 after a long and brutal dance with cancer. After he had his initial surgery I visited him in Mayday Hospital, Croydon. The ward was full of men of his age and background, all smokers, all blighted by the same affliction. Fifty years of factory work left a lattice of cracks on his hands that were hardened with calluses. Standing at a machine for ten hours a day had thickened his ankles and weakened his knees. The regimes of factory work left traces on the worker's body not always amenable to the naked eye but all too plain in the failing bodies in that hospital ward room. Like Engels' famous invocation of social murder, the illnesses found on this ward were the work of similar worldly perpetrators – bad working conditions, poor diet and an industry that profits from the sale of what my father called 'cancer sticks'.

As a young man things had been so very different. He had fancied himself as a bit of a 'spiv', inured to the world and style of the south London gangsters. There are pictures of him posing with his great friend Johnny Graham in the back garden of his mother's terraced home. They are dressed in double-breasted suits, silk ties and long-collared shirts. Dad and Johnny used to get on the train at East Croydon and head for the jazz clubs of Soho, or the boxing gyms, often over pubs, on the Old Kent Road, or to go dog racing at Catford. He carried with him always the humour and love of life that he found in those places.

He served in the Navy but he did not plot his travels in his skin. He forbade my brother and I to have tattoos even though we both wanted them. He 'laid down the law' in the Lacanian sense of a symbolic order, but for him tattoos signified self-damnation and class stigma and undermined his aspirations for post-war social improvement.[19] Like many, his image of a 'step up' was to move to the edge of the city, to the large council estates that offered the promise of better conditions and amenities. In such concrete citadels, working-class culture was deracinated and displaced. Yet, even here the legacy of the past was registered on the working-class body in code.[60] Memories do not have to be consciously held in order for them to be socially alive.[61] Rather, they can furnish a structure of feeling, while remaining elusive, even to those who inhabit them. Our father would not tolerate any carping about progress. For him it was simple. He wanted for his family better than he had known. Towards the end of his life, he looked on in bewilderment as his granddaughter Vicki presented a new tattoo on a more or less monthly basis.

The overwhelming sense of loss following his death consumed us all in different ways. For my brother Ken – Vicki's father – the particular nature of his death cast a shadow over his own future. He is a sheet metal worker and for many years he worked in a factory next door to his father. Now he travels all over the London area, repairing steel structures and erecting steel security gates. The industrial order of Fordist production is fast disappearing in London and a report in 2006 estimated that, between 2002 and 2016, manufacturing employment will fall by 30 per cent from 285,000 to 199,000 jobs.[62] The routines of Ken's working life provide an indicator of how London's economy is shifting: his work ranges from repairing kitchens in fast food outlets like McDonald's, to erecting security gates for warehouses and office complexes for designers and information technology companies.[63] In 2004 the Prime Minister's Strategy Unit produced the London Project Report, which defined the capital's economy as 'rooted in human talent, and expressed through knowledge-based, creative and cultural industries, including tourism'.[64] The capital in the twenty-first century is a place to create knowledge and design things rather than manufacture them.

Following our father's death, Ken went through a period of wearing his clothes, even his glasses. He inhabited his father's absence, in a literal way. He filled out his father's clothes with his own body and carried his garb with an almost identical language of movement and social orientation. Father and son possessed what Bourdieu calls a shared *bodily lexis*.[65]

Like many families in London we have a small caravan on the south coast, a place we have returned to for summer holidays since 1957. In the 1980s my parents brought a second-hand van to Norman's Bay and in the months after our father's death we continued to visit. It was almost impossible to be there. Every place resonated with his absent presence – the beach, the sea and the seawall where he stood to smoke a cigarette and look out on to the waves with the wind pushing back his mane of silver hair. Then one warm summer afternoon Ken said he had something to show me. He rolled up his shirtsleeve and there, on the top of his shoulder, was a tattoo, a graphic imagos, consisting of a swallow in flight, holding a scroll in its beak and on that fleshy parchment was inscribed three letters – DAD (see Figure 7).

The tattoo names the object of an illocutionary love. As Alfred Gell points out, this apparently individual choice is in fact elicited by others. In Ken's case they are his family, those closest to him and the spectre of his father. It symbolizes a love that was rarely, if ever, brought to speech, yet it is named. It *is* the name. Psychoanalyst Jacques Lacan claims that from the very beginning of their lives, children have distinct relationships to their fathers. This stands in contrast to the immediate physical connection to their mothers that is fashioned at birth and through nursing. Children develop a corporeal relation to their mother, while they learn of their relationship to their fathers through language and the word. As Daniel Schwarz concludes, 'the father's relationship to the child is thus established through language and a system of marriage and kinship – names – that in turn is basic to [the] rules of everything'.[66] The veracity of these claims is not the issue here, for what Lacan alerts us to is the symbolic weight contained in the name of the father. The father stands not only for paternity and love but also for a social or moral order.

The inscription of 'Dad' on Ken's shoulder points to the complexities of that moral order. Remember, his father had prohibited him from having such inscriptions. Yet, it is precisely through this debarred line that Ken memorializes his father. Ken's tattoo both carries his father's memory and defies parental authority. In the end, our father lives in part through the breaching of the law that he 'laid down to us' as children. Our father could on occasion be fierce and harsh and, inevitably, as a young man Ken had fallen foul of his discipline. His tattoo thus contains both sweetness and pepper.

Five years on from our father's death, Ken has become like him, not in terms of physical characteristics, or in the superficial surfaces of appearance. The invisible tattoos have been imprinted on his thought, action and conduct. This, to me, is something of a miracle and a comfort. We had not spoken of this. That is until I brought my day-job home and turned myself into a putative family ethnographer. All the emotions, palpable support and love demonstrated through the bereavement were never named. I want to suggest that this is much more than a family matter. It can be read as an example of the complexity of working-class

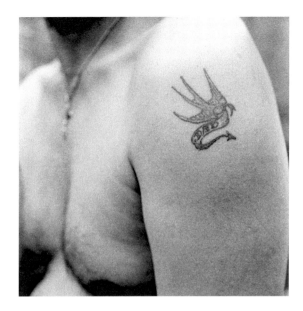

Figure 7: Ken's memorial
(© by Paul Halliday)

emotional lives, which have so often been viewed as indifferent, expressionless and lacking sensitivity.

Within white working-class contexts, men, and, to a lesser degree, women possess a kind of laconic halter when it comes to overfamiliarity. This is certainly the case in south London and its hinterlands, and may be specific to the history of this region and the class cultures that have taken hold. This is not quite the process of 'making the self smooth', or levelling out the internal and external fluctuations of emotion that Clifford Geertz described so vividly in the context of Java.[67] Rather, it is an imperturbable mask that holds still in the face of loquaciousness of any kind. Displays of overfamiliarity and easy affection are met with chilled scepticism. This in part has acted as a defence against external approaches, be it in the form of opportunistic politicians – on the left or the right – or the moral scrutiny of social workers and bourgeois professionals.

The language of love is articulated through acts and gestures within an embodied realm. Here the common-sense maxim 'actions speak louder than words' takes on a literal significance. The danger inherent in this unspoken love is that its communication might be distorted and not received clearly. These embedded emotional affinities can be misinterpreted, assumed, looked past or taken for granted. My essential point is that the lack of speech is not necessarily an indicator of an absence of love. More than this, the expression and communication of love needs to be understood through the range of verbal and non-verbal modalities.

Conclusion: The Colour in the Portrait

In this chapter I have tried to explain that which is not easily accessible to the written word. The key argument has been that within white working-class contexts the body becomes a figure on which emotions, affinities and devotions are inscribed. I have tried to show, through examining the photographs contained here, that the tattooed marks on these bodies contain complex, metonymic interconnections, meanings and symbolism. The colouring of these portraits – which is what I have tried to do through writing – is partial because each contains an enigma. Trying to find meaning in them is like grasping a handful of sand; most of the grains of truth slip through the fingers.

For Lacan, the act of signification, or any form of representation, is inherently unstable. It is what Kirsten Campbell has termed, 'the slide in the sign' or *glissement* in Lacanian language, that is, 'the process in which the signified constantly slides beneath the signifier'.[68] As Lacan argues, it is impossible to 'say it all' because ultimately 'words fail'. Part of this deficit is identified by Raymond Williams in what he calls the slide towards the past tense in cultural analysis and what he refers to as 'fixed forms of understanding'. The complexities of the present resist the categories we use to understand them: something always escapes and remains opaque.

> Perhaps the dead can be reduced to fixed forms, though their surviving records are against it. But the living will not be reduced, at least in the first person; living third persons may be different. All the known complexities, the experienced tensions, shifts, and uncertainties, the intricate forms of unevenness and confusion, are against the terms of the production and soon, by extension, against social analysis itself.[69]

This inadequacy in the act of representation is made all the more apparent here, given that the people contained in this study are my immediate family and close friends. What I have offered is very much a first-person narrative in the way Raymond Williams characterizes it. The portraits are inherently incomplete. They are sketches rather than portrayals in which all the shades of experience are detailed. But it is more difficult to indulge in quick judgements and crass sociological objectification when the subjects are your loved ones. This has been a lesson in itself. But the inevitable failure in the act of representation is not necessarily defeat. Ethnographic representation should aspire to better kinds of failure, to paraphrase Samuel Beckett's evocative phrase. This involves being open to the complexities and incomplete nature of present-tense experience, while at the same time avoiding reduction, fixing and closure.

Perhaps this draws attention to the ethics of thinking itself. If thinking is a moral act, what kind of moral act is it, specifically when it involves intimate dialogue of the kind described here?[70] Pierre Bourdieu has written that listening involves an intimacy that is both intellectual and emotional.

> Thus, at the risk of shocking both the rigorous methodologist and the inspired hermeneutic scholar, I would say that the interview can be considered a sort of *spiritual exercise* that, through forgetfulness of self, aims at a true *conversion of the way we look* at other people in the ordinary circumstances of life. The welcoming disposition, which leads one to make the respondent's problems one's own, the capacity to take idle persons and understand them just as they are in their distinctive necessity, is a sort of *intellectual love…*[71]

The portraits I have offered are themselves outlined through love; these pages are written with it. Making the 'respondent's problems one's own', in this case, contains an immediacy because it has, through thinking, involved a healing and reckoning with personal loss and bereavement. Ken is my brother and his father was my father. But I hope that this discussion also resonates with Bourdieu's contention that sociology should be about a process of *conversion* and transformation in the way we look at other people and their bodies.

The paradox of working-class tattooing is that it can, and does, mark out the painted body as a target for class stigma and prejudice. My argument throughout has been that contained within these inscriptions are complex emotions and affinities. Sue Benson has argued that the conception that the body can be remade and fashioned is a powerful one today. Yet, the tendency to think of the body as something that can be styled and controlled contains a broken promise. Tattooing and other forms of body culture bring this paradox into clear view.

> For in truth we do not own our bodies, they own us, that the only thing that is certain about our bodies is that they will let us down, that in the end they cannot be mastered or bent to our will. In this sense what these practices bring into sharp focus is the *impossibility* of Western ideas about body and self, and of these fantasies of permanence, control autonomy that they seek to negotiate.[72]

The lines in these tattoos touch permanence but cannot grasp eternity. This has a double consequence for working-class expression because this is often the only medium through which their stories are told. There is no place for them, and no prospect of what Derrida calls a 'hospitable memory'.[73] As the cadavers disappear, the traces of their embodied history, of life and love, are lost. They pass through hospital wards to the crematoria, their names remembered in floral wreaths and the inscriptions made on young flesh that will in turn grow old.

As Zygmunt Bauman pointed out, the most important things often remain unsaid and this chapter has emphasized the need to pay attention to the realm of embodied social life that operates outside of talk. Here visual sociology and photography enables us to access and represent the communications written on the body. However, the photographs do not speak for themselves and in order to make sense of them we need to be alert to the interplay between what is inside and outside the frame. The form of sociological attention being developed in my work is trained on listening to what is said but also focusing on what is shown. I suggest a kind of attention that translates across the senses where hearing is looking and looking is hearing.

Notes

1   Debbie Back treated this patient in the winter of 2000 and I am grateful to her for sharing his story.

2   Jones, C. P. 'Stigma and Tattoo.' In *Written on the Body: the Tattoo in European and American History*, edited by Jane Caplan. London: Reaktion Books, 2000: 1.

3   Caplan, Jane, ed. 'Introduction.' In *Written on the Body,* edited by Caplan.

4   Guest, Harriet. 'Curiously Marked: Tattooing and Gender Difference in Eighteenth-century British Perceptions of the South Pacific.' In *Written on the Body,* edited by Caplan.

5   Gustafson, Mark. 'The Tattoo in the Later Roman Empire and Beyond.' In *Written on the Body,* edited by Caplan.

6   MacQuarrie, Charles W. 'Insular Celtic Tattooing: History, Myth and Metaphor.' In *Written on the Body,* edited by Caplan.

7   Gell, Alfred. *Wrapping in Images: Tattooing in Polynesia.* Oxford: Clarendon Press, 1993: 10.

8   Rediker, Marcus. *Between the Devil and the Deep Blue Sea: Merchant Seamen, Pirate, and the Anglo-American Maritime World.* Cambridge: Cambridge University Press, 1987.

9   Modiano, Patrick. *The Search Warrant.* London: The Harvill Press, 2000: 23.

10   Hamish, Maxwell-Stewart and Ian Duffield. 'Skin deep devotions: religious tattoos and convict transportation to Australia.' In *Written on the Body,* edited by Caplan: 133.

11   Harris, Mick. Personal Communication, 15 December 2000.

12   Gell. *Wrapping in Images:* 37.

13   Foucault, Michel. *Discipline and Punish: The Birth of the Prison.* London: Allen Lane, 1977: 25.

14   Foucault, Michel. *Aesthetics, Method, and Epistemology.* London: Allen Lane, 1994: 375.

15   Foucault. *Aesthetics, Method, and Epistemology:* 376.

16   Glatzer, Nahum Norbert, ed. *The Collected Short Stories of Franz Kafka.* London: Penguin Books, 1988: 144.

17   Glatzer. *The Collected Short Stories of Franz Kafka:* 145.

18   Levi, Primo. *If This is a Man/The Truce.* London: Abacus, 1987: 76.

19   Phillips, Susan A. 'Gallo's Body: decoration and Damnation in the Life of a Chicano Gang Member.' In *Ethnography* 2, no. 3, 2001: 369-70.

20   Phillips. 'Gallo's Body': 384.

21   *BBC Radio 4,* The Sunday Papers, Sunday 4 August 2001.

22   'True Hair to the Chav Throne.' *The Croydon Guardian,* Wednesday 26 January 2005.

23   Burchill, Julie. 'Yeah but, No But, Why I am Proud to Be A Chav.' In *The Times,* 15 February 2005, www.thetimes.co.uk/tto/life/article1722148.ece.

24   See www.chav-scum.co.uk and www.chavtowns.co.uk.

25   Wallace, Mia and Clint Spanner. *Chav!: A User's Guide to Britain's New Ruling Class.* London: Bantam Books, 2004: 211.

26   See Basil Bernstein. 'Social Class, Language and Socialisation.' In *Power and Ideology in Education,* edited by Jerome Karabel and A. H. Halsey. New York: Oxford University Press, 1979, and Basil B. Bernstein. *The Structuring of Pedagogic Discourse.* London: Routledge, 1990.

27   Weil, Simone. 'Human Personality.' In *The Simone Weil Reader,* edited by George A. Panichas. New York: David McKay Company, Inc., 1977: 332–3.

28   Bauman, Zygmunt. *Liquid Love: On the Frailty of Human Bonds.* Cambridge: Polity, 2003: 2.

29   Tagg, John. *The Burden of Representation.* Basingstoke: Macmillan, 1988.

30   Berger, John and Simon McBurney. *The Vertical Line.* London: Artangel, 1999.

31   Merleau-Ponty, Maurice. *The Phenomenology of Perception.* London: Routledge & Kegan Paul, 1962: 206.

32   Merleau-Ponty, Maurice. *The Visible and the Invisible*. Evanston, USA: Northwestern University Press, 1968: 146.

33   Robson, Garry. *'No One Likes Us, We Don't Care.'* Oxford: Berg, 2000: 19.

34   Interview with author, 11 April 1996.

35   Interview with author, 11 April 1996.

36   Interview with author, 11 April 1996.

37   Interview with author, 11 April 1996.

38   Caplan, Jane. 'Introduction.' In *Written on the Body,* edited by Caplan.

39   Bale, John. *Landscapes of Modern Sport*. Leicester: Leicester University Press, 1994.

40   Tuan, Yi-Fu. 'Geopiety.' In *Geographies of the Mind: Essays in Historical Geosophy in Honor of John Kirtland Wright*, edited by David Lowenthal and Martyn Bowden. New York: Oxford University Press, 1975.

41   *The Sun*, 8 November 2001: 27.

42   Randall, Housk and Ted Polhemus. *The Customized Body*. London: Serpent's Tail, 1996.

43   bell hooks. *All About Love: New Visions*. London: The Women's Press, 2000: 3.

44   bell hooks. *All About Love:* 5.

45   *Nil By Mouth,* 1997, Twentieth Century Fox Film Corporation, written and directed by Gary Oldman.

46   Burchill, Julie. *The Guardian Columns 1998–2000*. London: Orion Publishing Group, 2001.

47   See Michael Collins. *The Likes of Us: A Biography of the White Working Class*. London: Granta Books, 2004.

48   Young, Toby. 'Action Man.' In *The Guardian,* G2, 16 January 2002: 3.

49   Young, Michael. 'Christmas Day Remembrance.' In *The Independent*, Tuesday 27 December 1988: 15.

50   Skeggs, Beverley. *Formations of Class and Gender*. London: Sage Publications, 1997: 83.

51   Skeggs. *Formations of Class and Gender:* 83.

52   Skeggs. *Formations of Class and Gender:* 83.

53   'The Ugliness of New Addington.' In *Croydon Advertiser,* 22 June 1956:1.

54   'The Politics of Housing', *The Suburban Press* 4, 1972: 2.

55   Fieldnote, 22 July 2001.

56   Bourdieu, Pierre. *Distinction: A Social Critique of the Judgment of Taste*. London: Routledge, 1986.

57   Bradley, James. 'Body Commodification? Class and Tattoos in Victorian Britain.' In *Written on the Body,* edited by Caplan.

58   Williams, Raymond. *Marxism and Literature*. Oxford: Oxford University Press, 1977.

59   Lacan, Jacques. *Écrits: A Selection*. London: Tavistock Publications, 1977.

60   Back, Les. 'Out of the Shadows.' In *Contagious*, edited by Daryll Bravenboer. London: Croindene Press, 2001.

61   Connerton, Paul. *How Societies Remember*. Cambridge: Cambridge University Press, 1989.

62   London Development Agency. *Production Industries in London: Strategy and Action Plan 2005–2008*. London: London Development Agency, 2006: 4.

63   See Fran Tonkiss. 'Between Markets, Firms and Networks: Constituting the Cultural Economy.' In *Market Relations and the Competitive Process*, edited by Alan Warde and Stan Metcalfe. Manchester: Manchester University Press, 2002, and Andy Pratt. 'New Media, The New Economy and New Spaces.' In *Geoforum* 31, 2000: 425–36.

64   Prime Minister's Strategy Unit. *London Project Report*. London: Cabinet Office, 2004: 7.

65   Bourdieu. *Distinction*: 474.

66   Schwarz, Daniel R., ed. *James Joyce's 'The Dead': A Case Study of Contemporary Criticism*. New York: Bedford Division of St. Martin's Press, 1994: 94.

67 Geertz, Clifford. 'From the Native's Point of View: On the Nature of Anthropological Understanding.' In *Interpretive Social Science: A Reader,* edited by Paul Rabinow and William M. Sullivan. Berkeley, Los Angeles: University of California Press, 1979.

68 Campbell, Kirsten. 'The Slide in the Sign: Lacan's Glissement and the Registers of Meaning.' In *Angelaki: Journal of the Theoretical Humanities* 4, no. 3, 1999: 135.

69 Williams. *Marxism and Literature:* 129–130.

70 Geertz, Clifford. *Available Light: Anthropological Reflections on Philosophical Topics.* Princeton, NJ: Princeton University Press, 2001: 21.

71 Bourdieu, Pierre. 'Understanding.' In *The Weight of the World: Social Suffering in Contemporary Society,* edited by Pierre Bourdieu et al. Cambridge: Polity Press, 1999: 614.

72 Benson, Sue. 'Inscriptions of the Self: Reflections on Tattooing and Piercing in Contemporary Euro-America.' In *Written on the Body,* edited by Caplan: 25.

73 Derrida, Jacques. *Specters of Marx: the state of the debt, the work of mourning, and the New International.* London: Routledge, 1994: 175.

NELE BRÖNNER

Ruth Behar

My Mexican Friend Marta Who Lives across the Border from Me in Detroit

Marta and I live a half hour away from each other, but there is a gaping-wide border between the corner house she and her family are borrowing from her brother-in-law in Detroit and my two-story Victorian house in a quiet, tree-lined neighborhood of Ann Arbor. Neither of us ever pretends that this border is inconsequential. Yet the circumstances of our lives have brought us at once so close and so far, and within that space we have managed to build a friendship.

It is June of 1993, and I am preparing for a return visit to Marta's hometown in Mexico, where David and I have lived, off and on, for ten years. She herself can't go back, because her husband Saúl has just lost his job and their economic situation is shaky. So this year I will be the one to hug her parents and sisters, and to spend afternoons chatting in the patio with her *abuelitos,* her beloved and frail grandparents.

Marta arrives with Saúl to drop off a Sear's catalogue for me to take to her family. And she brings their video camera to shoot some footage of my house. For Marta my house is a museum. She goes around talking into the camera as she points out highlights in our living room and dining room. "We come to this house a lot. Our friends like to invite us over," she says, chuckling.

My house is filled with books, embroidered cloths, and antique furniture; and there are clay pots, enameled trays, and bark paintings brought from Mexico. It is a house of many rooms, wood-framed windows, and a garden. I sometimes can't believe it is my house, bought with my own money. As a Cuban immigrant kid, I grew up in a series of cramped apartments in New York, so when Marta tells me she loves to come to my house, that it is her dream house, I understand, but feel odd that the things I have acquired are inspiring wanting and longing in someone else. She takes notice of anything new – a wicker chair, a used piano, a Turkish beaded good luck charm, new tiles in the bathroom with whimsical nopal cactuses, also brought with us from Mexico.

Marta focuses her camera on all of my Mexican wares. "Look at all the beautiful things from Mexico," she says into the camera. She seems to be displaying for her family back in Mexico all the Mexican things the anthropologist has in her house, which the Mexican herself, namely, Marta, doesn't want to have. Marta, for whom Mexico is her grandparents, her seven siblings, and her mother and father, who were always working not to become poor, desires none of these things; she dreams of packages filled with pretty white linens, edged in lace, that you order from catalogues, and she wants elegant, gold-trimmed porcelain dishes, the kind you can sometimes find on sale for fifteen dollars, service for four, at K-Mart.

I am always the one who phones Marta. When Marta decided to marry Saúl and come live with him in the United States, I made a promise to her parents and grandparents in Mexico that I would always look out for her on this side of the border. I haven't been able to explain to her family that another border separates us here.

"Marta, how are you?" I ask in Spanish, addressing her in the informal *tú*. We have spoken our native Spanish to one another since we met ten years ago in Mexico. We may both speak English to our sons, but our friendship is lived in Spanish.

"I'm fine. And you?" Marta always addresses me in the formal you, as *usted*. She won't let me forget that I am ten years her senior; that when we met in Mexico she was a young girl finishing high school and I was already a married woman embarking on a career as an anthropologist and writer. Even after seven years in the United States, and my continual requests that she address me as *tú,* Marta insists on maintaining certain formalities that acknowledge the age, cultural, educational, and class differences between us.

"And how is Saúl?"

"He's okay. He got that job teaching high school Spanish. Says he's going to earn almost as much as he used to at his old job. Says he's looking forward to the long summer vacations. We're just waiting for them to call about his physical exam." I have known Saúl for about as many years as I have known Marta. Born in the United States of Mexican parents, Saúl grew up in Michigan, working summers with his four brothers and their parents in the cherry, apple, and cucumber harvests. When I met Saúl, he was searching for his roots in the same Mexican town in which David and I were searching for a topic to study. He'd usually visit around Christmas, hosting lively *posadas* at the house of his mother's cousin, where the tamales were plentiful and a big piñata bulging with sweets was never lacking. On one of his first visits, when I met him, he came with a girlfriend, a *gringa* with long curly blonde hair; and years before, he had come with a different girlfriend, also a *gringa*.

But during the Christmas season in 1983, he came alone. Marta, who had won a scholarship to attend a state boarding school, was home on a vacation from her job teaching in a rural school. Her hair was permed, she wore a pink knit blouse and fitted pants, and danced an entire night with Saúl at a fifteenth birthday party, the *quinceañera,* of a cousin. Soon after, when he returned to the States, they wrote letters to each other every day. Two years later, they decided to get married, against the objections of Marta's father. He described Saúl, thirteen years older than Marta, as a *gallo,* an old rooster, who wanted the hand of a *pollito,* a little chick.

Marta and Saúl were married in a big church wedding in Mexico in December of 1985 and moved to East Lansing, where Saúl worked in the personnel department of Michigan State University. In the university setting, Marta met other women from Latin America and studied English. Saúl, who realized he had taken Marta away from her job, hoped she'd prepare to become a teacher of bilingual education. But Marta soon decided she wanted to have a child and, without letting Saúl know, she let him get her pregnant. What she hadn't expected was that it would happen so quickly.

Their son, Eduardo, was born in 1988, when Marta was twenty-three, and in 1989 they moved to the Detroit area, where Saúl found a better-paying job in a state government office. For the next three years they lived in a garden apartment in Romulus, under the flight paths of the Detroit Metro airport, where few families with children lived. Marta felt unsafe and stayed indoors all the time, shut within the four walls of their apartment, with her baby and the television as her only companions. Marta says she learned English watching soap operas. Later they moved to another apartment in Westland, where there were more families with children, and the stores were within walking distance. It was not yet Marta's dream house, but at least she felt less isolated.

Then Saúl lost his job. To save money he and Marta gave up their garden apartment and moved into his brother's house. It was a difficult moment, especially because they had taken on the added responsibility of caring for Marta's brother and sister, who had come from Mexico with all their papers in order thanks to Saúl's efforts. Polo and Lisandra planned to complete their last year of high school in the United States and then study in a community college. The two of them had learned English quickly and progressed rapidly in their schoolwork. Saúl was proud of them and hoped their presence would cheer up Marta, who had grown depressed and moody in her new surroundings.

"Guess what?" Marta suddenly announces. "I've signed up for a course. Saúl says it would be good for me. It's a course about relationships, about letting go of the anger you've been carrying around since you were a child. Do you know I still have dreams in which I get angry because my mother isn't home to take care of me?"

Women think back through their mothers, and, indeed, Marta wants to become a different kind of mother than her mother. Marta tells me that her adult self comprehends that her mother had to work hard, first as a peddler and then as a schoolteacher, to care for her eight children; but even so, she says with anguish, she can't forget how as a child she felt neglected and wished she could be wrapped inside her mother's arms, those arms which were always busy working. In the United States, Marta imagined she could become the mother she didn't have, the mother who would plan her pregnancy and be exclusively devoted to her child. And so she chose to have one child, Eduardo, for whom she has cared singlehandedly during the early years of his childhood. And she has chosen, too, to make it impossible to ever have another child.

It is October 1992, five months after Marta's hysterectomy. With some hesitation I have asked Marta if I can write about her operation for a conference on women's health. I fear that treating her as an anthropological subject will hurt our friendship, but Marta immediately agrees to let me write about her. She considers it an honor, she says, that I am interested.

We sit on her bed with the white lace coverlet. A mirror is behind Marta and I try not to look at my own face as I look at her. Little Eddy is in the living room playing with David, who has accompanied me on this trip because I don't like to drive to Detroit alone. The tape recorder is on the bed and I hold up the microphone toward Marta. We don't know that the tape recorder is not recording anything; only later, when I get home, will I learn that David forgot to put the batteries in the microphone.

On three sheets of lined loose-leaf paper, Marta has begun to write her life story in a few broad strokes. I read her handwritten words and notice how careful she has been to leave out anything painful; but her sense of solitude is profound and it surfaces, unwillingly, several times in her brief text, which ends in mid-sentence, with the words, "I have tried not to be an abnegated wife, but a …" She has held within herself all the pain of social and cultural displacement, all the tension of her rite of passage from virgin to wife, and all the anxieties of losing her womb so soon after becoming a mother.

Knowing that she planned to have only one, or maybe two children of her own, Marta tells me she tried to enjoy every moment of her pregnancy. It was a special time that she remembers with joy. But giving birth was a nightmare for her. At the hospital, when she became fully dilated, the doctors told her that the baby's head was too big and that they needed to perform a C-section. They had given her a spinal block for pain relief and later they put her under total anesthesia to perform the C-section. Saúl was not allowed to be present at the birth and the staff delayed bringing the baby to her. Apparently the anesthesiologist was sloppy, because after giving birth Marta suffered for four months from terrible headaches and body pains caused by the spinal block. She cries remembering how she could barely take care of Eddy at first. For Marta, having a C-section, especially one that was botched and alienating, made her feel that her womb wasn't worth much. She told me that the doctor who took out her uterus cut along the dotted line of her C-section scar.

Marta found the doctor who performed her hysterectomy, a board-certified obstetrician, in the phone book. She had already gone to two other doctors, both women, before seeing him. The two previous doctors, she felt, were unscrupulous in their desire for money; after learning what a good health insurance plan she had through her husband's job, they had immediately wanted to perform hysterectomies without even running a single test or analysis. As a rule she prefers women doctors, she says, because she's a Latina and finds it shameful to be examined by a man. But the doctor she found in the phone book impressed her enough that she put her trust in him. He's Cuban, she tells me, which I already know, cringing at the thought that Marta, in a subliminal way, may have put her trust in him because she's learned from me that Cubans are okay. I am holding the microphone that is taping nothing as she tells me that she wanted to have tests done and the Cuban doctor did them. She wanted to be sure she needed this operation and he convinced her she did. Her heavy menstrual bleeding had worried her since she was a young girl, but after giving birth, it had gotten worse. She had to rest during her periods and take iron; during those days, she fell behind on the cooking and cleaning and she didn't like that, because if the house was going to be her only responsibility, she wanted to do it well. The doctor told her if she went on bleeding so heavily one day she'd have a hemorrhage. He also told her that she had a tumor in her uterus, but after removing the uterus he admitted there was no tumor. He claimed her uterus was abnormally enlarged, that it had not shrunk back to its proper size after pregnancy.

Marta is beginning to question her doctor's advice and motives. She is not so sure anymore that he wasn't out for the money, too. And she recognizes that he's not so honest, perhaps, as she thought at first. When she tells him she's been gaining weight after the operation, he pretends it is her eating habits that are responsible; but later she finds out that it's very common for women who lose their uterus to put on weight. But what matters is her health, she says. It's nice not to be worried about her periods anymore or about getting pregnant. She couldn't have gone on taking iron pills forever. And if she is not going to have any more children anyway, then she really doesn't need her uterus. She's lucky, she tells me, that Saúl is educated and accepts her in her new wombless state. In Mexico, she says, there are men who won't have a woman who's had a hysterectomy; they claim those women aren't women anymore.

Marta needs to affirm to herself that her decision was a wise one. She thought about it for a year and she feels she explored her options by getting several medical opinions. She believes her health has improved, that she is really better, much better. But the loss of her uterus has made her aware of all her losses – of everything she has given up, everything she is giving up, to make a new life for herself and her family on this side of the border.

Listening to Marta, I am remembering how, a few years before, in Mexico, I held the delicate hand of her wispy *abuelita* and promised I would do everything in my power to protect Marta from the many perils of modernity on this side of the border. Ay, how I fear that I have failed miserably to live up to my promise. And this anguish runs deep into my own life. Marta had her hysterectomy a year after my mother had hers. When my mother was trying to make up her mind, she asked me for advice. Her daughter, the professor, would surely be able to tell her whether she really needed to have her womb cut out. But at the time I was so pathetically ignorant I encouraged my mother to go through with the operation. Only later, belatedly, uselessly, did I acquire the cruel knowledge that in the United States more unnecessary hysterectomies are carried out than in any other country in the Western world. Had my mother's hysterectomy been unnecessary? I no longer knew what to think, but I experienced painful daughter's guilt, shame, and self-hate, wondering if my mother's body had been sacrificed, with my complicity, to the surgeon's knife.

When Marta let me know her plans, I became distraught again. This time, with Marta, I was in a position of knowledge, even of too much knowledge, about hysterectomies. And I shared my doubts with her, urged her not to make too quick a decision. But I also questioned my desire to intervene. Was that the role I should be playing in our friendship? Did I really know what was best for her? Marta had made up her own mind with a strange sense of rational passion and tragic inevitability. She seemed to be marking her arrival on this side of the border with truly brutal retribution – which, sadly, was directed at herself. All I could do now was mourn with her, mourn her truly unbearable losses, and in that way help her to heal.

You know, Marta says to me, the last time she was in Mexico she and her mother were joking around and her mother called her a good-for-nothing. Those words – *"no sirves para nada"* – stung, and the pain was compounded when Saúl recently said the same thing to her, also as a joke. As she recounts this, Marta's eyes fill with tears. Marta was the second daughter; it was her sister, the eldest, who was always the smart one, always the favorite of her father. When she was in Mexico, her father told her how proud he was of her older unmarried sister for having gotten so far in her studies and achieving degrees in two fields. But he didn't say anything to Marta about being proud of her. She longs for greater affirmation from her parents, and yet her deepest wish is to someday bring them both to the United States and provide for them in their old age.

Marta left everything behind to come to the States with Saúl, but she didn't receive a very warm welcome from his family. When her mother-in-law suddenly developed an inexplicable illness, her father-in-law accused Marta of having used witchcraft to cause the illness; later he told Marta that Saúl didn't love her and that she was lucky he had paid any attention to her. One brother-in-law called her an Indian from the *rancho* because she refused to drink beer; another brother-in-law told her she was *"un perro entrenado"* (a trained dog), because she was so concerned to keep Saúl happy, having dinner on the table when he returned from work and setting his clothes out for him, neatly ironed, each morning.

She doesn't do those things for Saúl anymore, Marta says, because he never thanked her, never showed any appreciation. If Saúl thought he was bringing back a young and innocent Mexican wife to do all his housework for him, those days are over, she says, wiping her eyes, her face hardening.

As David and I drive back to Ann Arbor, I tell him about how Marta told me she often feels worthless, that her life isn't amounting to anything. Tears come into David's eyes; he says that's how he often feels.

In our relationship, the usual division of labor and power has been reversed. David has played the role of faculty wife, caring for our son, Gabriel, and doing the kind of secretarial work for me that male professors are always thanking their wives for in the acknowledgment section of their books. Most of the time, I am able to display gratitude for David's help on a more regular basis and to encourage him in his own work, but I have also been spoiled by the bargain prices he offers on his services; like my male counterparts, I've gotten into the habit of depending on certain unpaid labors from him. So, back at home, when I discover that the tape on which I am expecting to base my paper for the women's health conference hasn't come out, a paper that must be ready to present in a week, I break out in a merciless fury.

"Why did you give me that microphone in the first place? I've never used that silly thing before! How was I to know it needed its own battery? Aren't you the one who always handles that stuff? Now what am I going to do? I can't replicate the conversation I just had with Marta! I may as well forget about going to the conference. And my paper is one of the plenaries. Thanks to you, I won't be able to go!"

David's head sinks. "I'm sorry," he says. But I go on, repeating the litany of my complaints, even though I know I'll be able to piece my paper together from notes and memories. After a while he gets angry enough to say, "Well, next time, *you* get the tape recorder set up."

"That's very easy to say now, isn't it?"

"Look, if you don't like the way I do things, maybe I should just leave."

"You really love to press the anxiety button by threatening to leave just when I'm counting on you to take care of Gabriel. That's so cruel!"

In the afternoon the two of us go to our yoga class, where we pretend not to recognize one another and occupy different parts of the room as though we were strangers.

Sometimes anthropology comes too close to home.

A few days later we return to Marta's house with a functioning tape recorder. David goes off to look at computers and I stay with Marta and Eddy. Our conversation is not so intense this time because of Eddy's interruptions. At one point Marta takes Eddy in her arms and holds him tight. "I try to remember to do this at least once a day," she says. But later, he gets wilder, and trying to get her attention, he punches her in the belly. "I'll be right back," she says and goes into the bathroom with Eddy. I think I can hear her hitting him. Lisandra is back from her high school and comes in to entertain me. No, I can't believe she'd hit Eddy, her one and only. Would she?

Marta returns with Eddy and I can't read any clues in his face or hers. From the closet she pulls out her photo album, and we slowly turn the pages, looking at the pictures of her as a student, eyes gleaming with promise. Eddy points to a picture of Marta and says, "Stupid!" Marta calmly says to him, "Don't say that. Say chicken." Eddy points to the picture again and says, "Stupid!" Marta takes a deep breath and repeats, "Say chicken, Eddy, okay?" Her eyes look like they're starting to water. Finally, Eddy whispers "Chicken" and Marta says, "*Gracias,* that's better, Eddy."

Eddy soon tires of the pictures and rushes out to the living room to watch the cartoons on television. Lisandra, always good-natured, excuses herself and follows after him. Glad to be alone with me again, Marta returns to her closet and pulls out a stack of neatly folded, sparkling clean towels. "These are my towels," she says. "I don't let Saúl or my brother Polo use them. Polo has pimples and I don't want him staining my towels."

Then Marta pulls out a big plastic bag. It is full of letters, the love letters Saúl wrote to her from Minnesota, North Dakota, and Michigan in the two years of their romance. She reads from two of them: one letter is about his struggle to find work after deciding to leave Minnesota; the other is about how they should deal with the problem of getting married by the Catholic Church, given his family's conversion to Protestantism (but later, as Marta explains, it turns out that his grandmother had baptized him and there was no problem at all). He'd start his letters with *Amor mío* ("My love"), punctuating them constantly with those words. He wrote very lyrically and in correct Spanish. When he went to ask Marta's father if *he* would let her marry him, Saúl announced, "I have a great weight upon my heart," and her father said, "Forget the poetry and get to the point."

Saúl saved all her letters just like she saved all of his. But her letters are gone. Destroyed by her own hands. Why, I ask, unable to hide the disappointment in my voice. Marta says she just decided, one day, to tear them all up. She told Saúl she was going to do it. And all he said was, "Well, if that's what you want to do…"

Back in a small town in Mexico, in the front room where her *abuelitos* sleep, Marta's wedding dress hangs from a nail in the wall. The dress remembers her body. Remembers how she danced before she said good-bye. Waits for her.

NELE BRÖNNER

Moritz Ege

Carrot-Cut Jeans:
An Ethnographic Account of Assertiveness,
Embarrassment and Ambiguity in the Figuration
of Working-Class Male Youth Identities in Berlin

Introduction

Adapting Georg Simmel's classic reflections on fashion, Daniel Miller and Sophie Woodward (2007: 341–2) have suggested that the near-global ubiquity of jeans offers people different ways of negotiating the conflicting sociocultural forces of conformity and individuality. In Woodward's British study, for instance, using a familiar and hardly spectacular example, jeans provided a 'relief from the burden of mistaken choice and anxious self-composition' that women continuously felt (Miller and Woodward 2007: 343). In terms of experience, the authors argue, such conflicting forces manifest in locally differentiated 'genres of anxiety'. With an anthropological sensibility both for the grain of experience and for local-global dynamics, they call for inquiries into specific versions of such genres, from the vantage point of this particular type of clothing, denim, and for compiling 'the responses that populations forge for themselves in dealing with certain contradictions of modernity' (Miller and Woodward 2007: 348). This chapter is a contribution toward this end. It engages ethnographically with one such situation, the popularity of a specific type of denim, the carrot-cut (high-waist pants that fit comparatively tight around the behind and the crotch, widen a bit toward the knee, and narrow again toward the hem – loosely resembling the shape of the vegetable) and a specific brand, Picaldi Jeans, among a large number of boys and young men in Berlin (and in Germany more widely), first as an ethnic youth practice, and then increasingly in connection with German 'gangsta rap'.

In depicting the practices and distinctions within this context, I also take up the notion of 'anxiety' and widen it into the social field, taking into account other people's responses to and judgements of the style represented by those jeans. These responses become quite heated, as this subcultural style involves issues of assertiveness, deviance, racism, and class contempt or even disgust.[1] While this brief analysis provides no more than a snapshot of this phenomenon, the overall project is undertaken in order to contribute to an understanding of the cultural processes which co-constitute post-working-class identities and figures (see below) within an increasingly diverse European society in which socioeconomic forces and an activating, neoliberalizing welfare state have made the fault lines of social inequalities – both in terms of class and ethnicity – increasingly visible.[2] In the language of public discourse, this concerns the joint problematic of 'immigrant integration' (Integration von Ausländern) and the emergence and consequent social management of a 'new underclass' (cf. the policy debate pushed forward by, for instance, Nolte 2004) in post-Fordist times through increasingly disciplinary-paternalistic types of citizenship.

In the first section of this chapter, I briefly lay out the situation in which these local 'genres of anxiety' arise. This involves some aspects of local migrant youth cultural history and aesthetics, developments within the genre of rap music internationally, and the transnational history of a small business. For the sake of concreteness, I also thickly describe some of the ways in which people wear those jeans and their differential relations with other options. The second section takes the form of a case study in which I portray one individual person, in order to represent some of the complexities and life-world relevancies. On the level of experience, I highlight the motive of *ambiguity* with regard to toughness and deviance which this person communicates and reflects and which, in my analysis, plays a large role in the overall cultural dynamics surrounding the 'Picaldi style'.[3] The third section takes up some of the ways in which other, more middle-class or respectability-oriented people view the jeans and the style – and I use this term broadly – they have come to stand for. This touches on the politics of labelling and *embarrassment* more broadly, as they relate to contemporary constellations of culture, class, ethnicity, and gender – seen through an analytical lens of classificatory cultural dynamics (Bourdieu 1984; Neckel 2003) and figuration: I take the concepts of cultural figures and figuration, which obviously have an extensive intellectual history, mainly from the American anthropologist John Hartigan who states that 'figures call attention to the way people come to consider their identities in relation to potent images that circulate within a culture.' In Germany, one crucial ascription in this context is the term 'Proll', which has been in use since the 1970s. Connotationally, the word retains its etymology (the proletariat, the working-class), but its denotational meaning is primarily behavioural and performative. Dictionaries list 'Prolet' as a 'person who lacks manners' and 'Proll' as a 'coarse, uneducated, vulgar person' (Duden 1999: 3024). These terms are being used in shifting and imprecise ways, which indicate, as I will argue, a number of uncertainties or anxieties. While the Berlin case is in some respects unique even within Germany, similar sociocultural processes of 'figuration' are taking place in many European countries, the most well-known being the case of the 'chav' figure in the UK, which emerged around 2004 (Tyler 2008).

Carrot-cut Jeans: From 'Saddle' to 'Zicco', from Diesel to Picaldi

As so often, the narrative is a part of the phenomenon. Picaldi's story is a part of local lore, transmitted by word-of-mouth and through a few journalistic accounts. Picaldi's carrot-cut jeans[4] are based on a denim model by Diesel Jeans ('Saddle'), which has been in continuous demand from, among others, youth and young adults with Turkish, Arab and other migrant backgrounds, since at least the mid-1980s, but has been considered outdated at best by many other style-conscious young people, and the press and the fashion world more generally, for a long time. In the late 1990s, before Diesel stopped selling this model, it was copied and re-branded by a small-scale local retailer, Unplugged, who ordered a batch of this design from an Istanbul-based manufacturer, named Picaldi, which had been founded in 1988, but hadn't been producing that type of jeans. Since then, the retailer's store in Berlin-Kreuzberg has grown into a small retail chain with twelve stores, an online dealership, and a handful of franchises in other cities. Moreover, Picaldi has been transformed, in Germany, from an obscure manufacturer's name, which was typeset to resemble a famous brand, into a relatively well-known brand of its own, albeit a controversial one.[5]

In many arenas of urban social interaction, the type of jeans in general, the carrot-cut ('Karottenschnitt', see below), and the brand in particular acquired the status of a marker of both ethnic and lifestyle identity among boys and young men with Turkish, Arab and other immigrant backgrounds, most of whom come from working-class, relatively low-income families.[6] It plays a significant part in creating identities within adverse circumstances. Many customers describe their own outfits as 'gangster style' or 'gangsta style', referring to imagined or real connections to organized crime, the shadow economy, and gangsta/gangster figures in various registers of international popular culture. Another term that is frequently used is 'Kanakenstyle', which takes up a partly re-signified, but still offensive, racist insult. In its initial advertising and store decoration, Picaldi built on gangster references, putting up 'Scarface' screenshots, and stressed their cheap prices, comparing themselves, tongue-in-cheek, to a discount supermarket chain ('Nix Aldi, Picaldi!'). Picaldi's jeans were sold much cheaper than Diesel's 'Saddle', at about 35 euros or half the price.

Picaldi found a second major group of dedicated customers, largely working-class, white German young men in the former East (of the city and the country), many of whom live in areas with a small presence of immigrants, relatively low average incomes, a high unemployment rate. The spread or diffusion of this specific style from an immigrant, lower or working-class setting to an autochtonous lower or working-class group can be described as transversal in character in that it crosses the social field, bypassing the symbolic centre. On the face of it, this combination of niche markets seems surprising, given the prevalence of anti-immigrant and racist sentiments among the latter group. In the case of Picaldi's original customer base, this *type* of outfit was in fashion long before the company picked them up. The stylistic practice and inventiveness seems thus relatively autonomous from commercial strategies. In the East German case, there exists a specific continuity regarding milieu-specific taste preferences, tied to masculine body images, movement sequences, and overall style in the presentation of self. This partly explains the popularity of this type of denim, and the brand that has come to stand for it, across an ethnic line that is otherwise much harder to traverse.

In socioeconomic and occupational terms, Picaldi's customer base is somewhat diverse, but it is predominantly – though certainly not exclusively – recruited from the working class and lower middle class, and, in terms of the education system, from the vocationally oriented middle and high schools *(Hauptschulen, Realschulen, Berufsschulen)*. Both the views of many Picaldi employees I interviewed and a small customer survey (with about 100 respondents) I completed in late 2007 confirm this assumption. Much to the chagrin of many among the company's leaders and employees, in the view of outsiders and in various media outlets, 'Picaldi' has come to stand much more narrowly for an 'underclass' of welfare recipients and violent offenders; the *Frankfurter Allgemeine Zeitung,* for instance, illustrated a reporting piece on living conditions of unemployment/welfare-recipients *(Hartz IV)* with the high price of a pair of Picaldi jeans, and various other articles in the press reiterated such associations.[7]

A Type of Jeans: Shapes and Distinctions

None of this is independent of the object in question itself – its form, the aesthetics of the male body it shapes, and the relational position of this type of jeans among other available options that are intentionally *not* chosen. This type of jeans, which Picaldi markets under the name 'Zicco' (and many other names for individual models), is often called 'carrot-cut' *(Karottenschnitt)*.[8] It is a high-waist pant, which makes for a higher fit than other denim cuts. It fits relatively tightly around the behind and the crotch, it widens toward the knee, and it narrows again toward the hem.[9] Compared with other men's carrot-cut jeans, these features are especially pronounced in the Zicco. Over time, Picaldi also introduced a wide variety of colours, dyes, appliqués and prints, as well as some other fabrics such as beige or light blue corduroy.

Most salespeople agree that the Zicco is made to be worn rather high, on the waist. Depending on the wearer's physique and the combination with other clothing items, this can make for different looks; many 'big guys' wear the jeans 'high', as originally intended by the designers, and they wear knit sweaters or sweatshirts with a waistband, maybe even tucked into the jeans, and/or a bomber or college/baseball jacket. Doing so supports the V-effect on the upper body, the stress upon narrow waistline and broad shoulders. This 'pumps up', as people say *(es pumpt auf)*,

Picaldi advertisements from 2004/2005

the trousers seem sportive *(sportlich)*, masculine *(männlich)* and figure-accentuating *(figurbetont)*, as most salespeople and customers put it in in-store conversations. The men's appearance is one of being 'broadly built' *(breit gebaut)*, 'like Michelin men', as a designer calls it, laughingly. (I will return to the character of such laughs.) The overall look is somewhat related to that of a sweat pants or the type of lighter pants that bodybuilders often wear. With their skinnier legs and narrower shoulders, many customers, especially the younger ones, lack the muscular physique needed to fill out the trousers, as it were, but they nonetheless wear them high-waisted. The fabric, which isn't very heavy in most models, dangles a bit and is, for instance, blown back by the wind. The jeans seem wider. This results in a different body appearance which, however, remains tied to the scheme mentioned above. As a Picaldi spokesperson put it in an interview: 'In those jeans, one automatically has an imposing appearance: muscular thighs, good behind, stately pace. That highlights the masculine aspect.'[10] Many, however, wear t-shirts that aren't tucked in, or sweaters and jackets without a waistband, which results in a less obvious look.[11]

The second option for wearing the Zicco jeans is to buy them in a larger size. This, of course, makes the fit looser, and one can wear the jeans lower, on the hip. Worn low, they are almost reminiscent of baggy pants, without being quite as wide and long. The aforementioned taste-predispositions in different groups are

Zicco, worn rather low; Picaldi catalogue spring/summer 2008, p. 6

remarkable in themselves, as they fundamentally contradict many accounts of tendencies toward postmodern classlessness in youth culture. However, these traditions might not have been relevant to this extent had they not been reinforced by other, converging developments within hip hop/rap music, which played a crucial role in the process of figuration. This markedly verbal-discursive genre, by now the dominant idiom for large parts of youth culture and split up into a variety of sub-scenes, has been crucial to Picaldi's unexpected expansion. Picaldi jeans became discursively entwined with a few commercially successful local rap artists, most of them in the gangsta rap mould. In this process, the brand has not only been popularized, it became tied up with a distinction integral to these rappers' confrontational mode of self-fashioning.

I cannot do justice to this scene, its aesthetics, or its politics here. In the early years of the decade, the focus of national attention shifted to the Berlin scene. To put it somewhat crudely, a widely adopted stance there was that the previously dominant scenes in German rap were doing hip hop in an ultimately inauthentic[12] way ('All MCs are gay in Germany', 'Alle MCs sind schwul in Deutschland', as Kool Savas put it),[13] whereas Berlin rappers had both fewer politically correct inhibitions and better rap skills and also, in many cases, an authenticating 'street' background. One version of this self-positioning motive, put forth by Bushido most prominently, concerned clothing: in this view, just like others lacked the experiential background that would qualify them for 'authentic' rap, they put on American-style baggy jeans, 'fake' costumes, whereas 'real' street-savvy gangsters and hustlers wore brands such as Cordon and Picaldi. This distinction also plays out on the level of shape and physique. Straight-cut baggy pants are famously worn 'low' on the hip or, more often, further down, so that the behind can hardly be made out. From shoes to shoulders, the silhouette has the shape of an A (as in the shape of the classic graffiti character type with shoes larger than the head) rather than a 'carrot' below the belt and a V above it, as with the carrot-cut: Wearing a carrot-cut, one still has 'an ass in one's pants' *(einen Arsch in der Hose),* as a German idiom, referring to courage and self-assertion, goes.[14] In this context, then, there is something like an antagonistic relationship between the carrot-cut and baggy jeans – however serious or playful this antagonism is imagined. The differential relation between the carrot-cut and straight-cut jeans, in contrast, derives primarily from a sequence, not an antagonism; here, biographical phases and status passages come into play. Many of Picaldi's customers, by an age between sixteen and twenty-two, choose to give up their

Ziccos and pick 'straight cuts', which may signal an overall change in style and attitude. This distinction reflects emic categories rather than the overall classification language in the denim industry.

Tarek's Case

Given this background, what does the life-world relevance of these jeans consist of? Which distinctions and what forms of togetherness are being created, upheld, challenged or broken down in this process? What, specifically, characterizes the predominant 'local genre(s) of anxiety'? In order to approach these questions and chart out some answers on the level of experience, I choose a narrative case-study approach. The person I want to focus on is a young man I met in the course of field research, Tarek M., who is twenty years old. While he should not be considered an all-round 'typical representative' of a social group or a habitus, but rather a case of complexity, an *homme pluriel* (cf. Lahire 2001), I argue that his case does indeed exemplify some intersubjective dynamics that in part constitute the overall context.

Tarek M. was born and raised in a relatively 'quiet' district on the south-west side of Berlin to a Lebanese father and a German mother, both of whom run a small grocery store in the neighbourhood. He is the youngest of four siblings. In the year in which Tarek and I have been meeting every once in a while, he has been in a difficult overall situation in terms of the transition from school to work. He mostly lives with his parents and he helps out in his parents' store, for which he receives no pay. He has not been able to secure the car salesman apprenticeship he wishes to take up, and he failed the entry exam at the Mercedes-Benz factory, where only a few applicants succeed every year.

Symbolic Boundaries and Social Relations

With regard to the style-identity-place-nexus, Tarek recalls the big change that occurs at the transition from primary to secondary school. In seventh grade, students enter a secondary school, an *Oberschule,* and they become tracked into different schools according to their grades and the teachers' verdict on their abilities, which brought him to a *Hauptschule,* the lowest-achieving option out of the three school types. There one inevitably meets people from other areas and begins to make spontaneous classifications, affinities and alliances based on style, among other things, he says. At that point, in Tarek's class, there was a clear break, socially and spatially, between those who were considered 'Germans' and those who were informally designated as 'foreigners' (i.e. descendants of recent immigrants, many of whom do not have German citizenship), which registered in different ways, for instance in seating arrangements. The 'Germans' made up about two-thirds of this class. Simultaneously, the distinction between the cool ones and the others became important. First of all, in his view, the emerging patterns of clothing among boys were very much an ethnic issue. 'You could recognize it by the clothing immediately. We were basically always dressed dark. Dark, casual *(lässig)*.' This distinction between two groups of students appears to be saturated with discourses, images, and affects from a variety of media, including film, music, and local narrative lore. The local discourse of Berlin rap at the time offered a particularly meaningful and attractive way of making sense of one's immediate surroundings. Furthermore, the primary to secondary school transition and the following years coincided with the rise of the Picaldi style and its increasing semanticization in the context of the hip-hop world. As I have shown above, Picaldi's carrot-cut jeans, as opposed to baggy jeans, became one crucially important marker of difference in that context. In this particular instance, then, subcultural and ethnic distinctions played themselves out very much in accordance with the playbook I outlined: 'The ones up front there [he points to the other group on a sketch], they had [somewhat disgustedly] skater-pants, skate sweaters and things like that,' as Tarek says.

The classroom situation he recollects highlights emotional and affective under-currents of such symbolic boundaries, which would suggest that there was some awareness of being in a socially low-status environment, and on a problematic track. The basic facts of discrimination were hard to ignore, from racist violence to small-scale resonances of structural exclusion such as, for instance, when he was the only one among his 'immigrant' peer group whose citizenship status allowed him to join a school trip abroad. On the other hand, on the experiential level, Tarek also speaks of a sense of privilege, prestige, aesthetics and power among 'the foreigners', *diese Macht bei den Ausländern,* echoing other ethnographic accounts. Even though he and his friends were a minority in terms of numbers, in his account, for a variety of reasons, they held interactional power (as opposed to institutional power), even dominance within the classroom, because of their assertiveness *(Durchsetzungsfähigkeit)* and cohesion. Furthermore, they possessed what can be called cultural attractiveness, which amounts to another form of symbolic power. It becomes confirmed, for instance, by the discursive framing in which Germans who took up style patterns (language, dress) of youth with migrant backgrounds were considered 'wannabeTurks', and it is confirmed through a variety of folklore and representations. The notion of male 'swagger', which recently underwent a revival in US popular culture language, captures the homologies that pertain between the quality of assertiveness, the shape of a 'masculine' physique, and the Picaldi carrot-cut (cf. Skeggs 2004). Many other aspects of this experiential world could be considered, such as the discursive motive of 'foreigners' cohesion versus Germans' individualization and dissociality (cf. Sutterlüty and Walter 2005, 194f), and one could attempt to trace back their causes. This, however, is not the place to do so. Here, I have touched on these experiences of simultaneous exclusion and assertiveness in order to specify the generic fact that cultural meanings of specific pieces of clothing, such as a pair of carrot-cut jeans, rely on emotions and affects that underlie symbolic boundaries. Furthermore, the cultural semiotics of identity and alterity, as they manifest in clothing codes, are enmeshed not only with symbolic and imaginary (subcultural, ethnic) communities, affinities, and figures, but also with 'real' groups, with interpersonal, interaction-based networks. The classroom is one important setting, as are scene-like forms of urban sociality, and of course family relations, friendships, and partnerships. The importance of family and friendship networks in this regard becomes apparent when we consider that for Tarek, as for most people in his social world, shopping represents a touchy subject because of his financial situation. Not having a significant source of income, he mostly depends on other people to spend money for him, and he has been doing so for a longer time than is generally thought proper. Hence, it is no longer his parents who supply his clothing, but his sister who buys both basics such as jeans and, when money is flush, more expensive brand-name items, such as much sought-after knitted-wool sweaters. In any case, this gift-giving is part of a both practised and idealized sense of family reciprocity: she wants his brother to look good; he is concerned with her well-being as well and, for instance, frequently serves as her driver. This is not to suggest that there are no or few family conflicts, but it shows some of the ways in which individual pieces of clothing carry not only sentimental value, but also materialize interpersonal relations of love, care, and control. Such relationships go beyond the family; in Tarek's case, as with many other people, clothes, such as jackets, sweatshirts, pants, watches, jewellery, are exchanged within an inner circle of friends. All of these aspects contribute to an understanding of the fact that the symbolic borderlines, despite their superficial and contingent nature, can matter deeply and why, in this context, identity is easily harmed.

Embodiment, Figuration, and Ethics

Another highly charged issue concerns the normative side of *relating to cultural types* more generally: imitation, mimesis, replication, emulation, or figuration. In a process that is discursive and physical, people construct their identities and shape their bodies in relation to the individuals, including stars and cultural heroes, they positively relate to: visually, aurally, affectively. While doing so comes – as we all know – with practical challenges, it also leads straight into the normative or even ethical dilemmas of conformity and individuality that pervade teenage life. Tarek, for instance, speaks animatedly about the relationship between the image that rap music projects, the reality that people live, and the role of such representations. In this respect, the last few years were a tumultuous time, given the fast rise of German gangsta rap. When it comes to rappers like Azad, Bushido and Massiv, many critical observers wonder whose commercial calculations are at play, who benefits, what are the representational costs (in terms of prejudices and stereotypes) and who bears these costs? Tarek, too, is concerned with the stereotypes that circulate about *Ausländer*. Almost whispering, he tells me he's been listening more closely, and critically, to rap lyrics and what they say. When it comes to the ways in which people embody the cultural figures that circulate through popular culture, he thinks, many people – young, male, youths with a migrant background, mostly, he means here – exaggerate in 'reflecting' *(widerspiegeln)* the music. The question – 'Pseudo-Gangstertum' – is much-debated within the wider circles of rap music, as is evident to anyone who has ever looked at a rap discussion forum or online video comment section (cf. Androutsopoulos 2005: 172). People say, Tarek continues, that Bushido 'reflects' the street. But really, it's the other way around: people follow Bushido's every move, they copy him in whatever he does. It makes him angry because people do stupid and violent things they wouldn't otherwise do, because they get into a sort of arms race in which people show how crazy, how *krass* they are, and furthermore (and this is a different, but important point), because in doing so, they are like sheep.

This practice of 'reflection', in Tarek's understanding, manifests both in that people increasingly carry knives and in specific forms of demeanour and clothing. 'Before there was this kind of rap, it wasn't like this: one in three wears an Alpha jacket, one in two wears an Alpha jacket. Back then, it was only the adults. The big ones. The bodybuilders and the like, bouncers and so forth, they had Alpha jackets. Now, suddenly, everyone has one.'[15] This streetwear arms race, as it were, indicates people's questionable, presumptuous, sheepish, and ultimately destructive imitations and identifications. He believes that in contrast to many others, he observes that music's malicious influence without distortion, and his stylistic practices are of a different nature. I challenge Tarek who, as I have come to notice in an earlier session, wears an Alpha Industries jacket himself, and I ask him in what sense exactly the people he talks about, the classic 'cultural dupes', are so different from himself. In reference to other people not being able to keep reality and fiction apart, I object that he and his friends seem able to do so, and from what I can tell, they also like to come across as tough, in some way or another. 'Oh, I know that difference. [It's a matter of upbringing, he says later.] But, you know, in order to scare people off *(abschrecken)*, I do what they talk about in music. You can scare people away. That's really the way it is.'

I ask him what situations he means, and he talks about meeting people from outside the city who, he believes, suppose that Berlin is really tough, *krass,* and are scared. He likes 'confirming' that stereotype. Then, automatically I act tough *(ich mache einen auf hart).* When they … why should I make myself smaller than I am, you know?' He then goes on to talk about people from distant neighbourhoods in the East, which are, as he points out elsewhere, known for the street dominance of white German working-class 'toughs' and anti-immigrant violence.

> You know, I don't know, or maybe from Marzahn or so … Then I say, then I don't present myself … We're no chicks *(Küken)!* Then I act tough *(ich mache einen auf hart).* 'I'm from Tempelhof', you know … That's normal. But I'm not flicking my knife or anything like that.

Obviously, some verbal posturing is going on here. At the same time, this going back and forth between rhetorical escalation and de-escalation points to an ambiguity that is not merely rhetorical. Significantly, he stresses the performative level when he uses phrases such as *einen auf hart machen.*[16] In youth language, there are many such metaphors that, in one way or another, differentiate between an intentional subject, on the one hand, and his or her performances, on the other hand. In those metaphors, the degree to which the subject controls or is controlled by that which is performed, or by the immersive quality of an imagination, varies.[17] Clothing is among a number of practices within this problematic. In a context of discrimination, racism, class disgust or negative classification, the question of embodying cultural figures is highly charged and relevant both practically and normatively. I will explicate this relation in the remaining section of this paper.

Ambiguity

'Is he a good boy? Isn't he a good boy? No one should know, that's how I want it to be,' Tarek says, smiling shyly. He's referring to a cliché *(guter Junge),* which has been used in rap quite a bit, and, in contracted form *(Ersguterjunge),* figures as the name of Bushido's rap label. Tarek's girlfriend Steffi uses a female adaption as a login on her laptop: *Siesgutesmädchen.* I had asked him about things and values that really matter to him. The context of this utterance is 'saving face' and maintaining a clean slate.

> T: That's the most important thing. But some people don't do that. Save face, I mean, and … For instance, in my case, it's like – nothing bad can be said about me. [M. Mhm.] About me … Maybe I'm doing bad stuff, but nobody knows. [M. laughs softly] You know? That's normal! As long as you don't know anything about me, you can't gossip. You can guess what I do. But you don't know, you don't know what I do. You know? [M: Okay.] That's always the question. Is he doing things? Is he not? Is he a good boy, is he not a good boy? [M. laughs softly] When it comes to me, this remains an open question. Nobody knows.
> M: You remain a riddle?
> T: For many, I do.
> M: And for you, it's important that it is that way?
> T: Yes. That's how it should remain.

There is an obvious situational irony at play: in this interview I, a researcher and outsider through age, ethnicity and various aspects of cultural background, try to find out various details about Tarek's life, and I am very much in the same position as the clueless anonymous 'you' (*du,* sometimes, agrammatically, 'he', *er*) that Tarek talks about. In that sense, his statements figure as commentary to our relationship as well as to his relationship to other people that surround him.

In both instances, this ambiguity is a question of the 'presentation of self' and 'impression management' (Goffman 1959) through figuration. Despite its obvious undertones of adolescent fantasy, there are at least two reasons why the ambiguity he produces through this form of impression management should not be trivialized: first, because there is some seriousness to the pole of toughness and violence within Tarek's life-world, not only in that people, including himself, do fight from time to time, but also in that there is some proximity to crime. Tarek's sister's boyfriend, for instance, was spending time in prison for violent assault as we were speaking, and through the wider network of friends and cousins, he knows a few people involved with 'Lebanese mafia' groups, which make up a significant segment of organized crime in the city, especially the drug trade. Secondly, and relatedly, ambiguity should be taken seriously as a cultural form because despite its obvious social costs, it has an *empowering* quality, which helps us understand what these jeans – as one element of a larger package – *are* on a subjective, experiential level.

Power, Spinoza famously posited, consists in the power to act, to affect and be affected (cf. Hardt 2007). The ambiguity Tarek intends to communicate, then, can be experienced as a small-scale, interaction-based form of power in both of these ways: in burdening alter with the question as to ego's violent or at least particularly assertive potential, ego 'affects' alter – scares him or her, for instance – and is himself affected, in that he gains options that arise from alter's confusion or passivity. For instance (and this happens quite frequently), ego gains the option of de-escalating – 'I'm just playing with you' – while seeming to never have made an effort to intimidate anyone in the first place. Such dramas are enacted on an everyday basis. They often take spatial form, such as when individuals or small groups of people demonstratively take up a disproportionate section of space and make others yield. Very abstractly speaking, ambiguity of this kind can be considered a form of interactional advantage.

Such poses and the concomitant experiences are not new, but their shape and significance depend on the specific cultural 'moments' of which they are elements.[18]

What matters (and varies) greatly, for instance, is the extent to which such poses are supported by the logics and imaginaries of contemporary global popular culture, their specific shape and politics, and their resonance with more local forms. In the case at hand, this ambiguity on the level of impression management, I argue, seems analogous to the ambiguous structure of the 'real' in gangsta rap, as it has been analysed by various critics. In the context of gangsta rap, for instance, the question almost automatically arises in what sense conflicts between rappers ('beef') are 'real'. Despite the fact that the social contexts of US and German gangsta rap are enormously different, much the same can be said for the 'real' and 'beef' in German gangsta rap. Were the shots fired in late 2007 (just before an album release) on Massiv 'real' or were they staged? To what degree of violence will 'beef' between rappers such as Kool Savas and Eko Fresh, or between Sido and Bushido, or between Fler and Bushido, lead? On the one hand, there certainly are 'literalist' interpretations of the genre, especially from young teenagers. On the other hand, many appreciate the model of a successful cynic. For many more people, however, this ambiguity (which, of course, isn't necessarily exactly seen as such) is in itself a large part of the pleasure of the genre. It can become appropriated as an attitude. Tarek's practices of impression management, which leave the question of whether he is a 'good boy' or 'not a good boy' intentionally open, provide a good example for such analogies. These two forms of ambiguity seem to be mutually reinforcing, inspiring and legitimating. Having that sort of resonance can be a powerful experience. A theoretical account is given by Brian Massumi who theorizes figures in an abstract but nonetheless evocative way, describing them, among other formulations, as 'a point of subjectification' and 'a gravitational pull around which competing orbits of affect and thought are organized' (Massumi 1998: 54).

Projected Embarrassment

Focusing on the 'inside' view, the experience of wearing the type of style that Picaldi is the most prominent part of, then, often involves such ambiguities, which hold an empowering quality for many. Specific projections of self-confidence are involved, as is a degree of aggressive assertiveness. For a causal *explanation* of these attitudes, one would have to consider the interplay of cultural dynamics and broader, structural social forces, and complete this account with other aspects of experience, which is an important task that I cannot accomplish here. Instead, in a provisional step of cultural analysis, I wish to further characterize the 'local genre of anxiety' by taking into account other, equally partial, but in some ways more socially powerful perspectives.

Picaldi is, as its press spokesperson puts it euphemistically, an 'emotional brand'. Many people actively dislike it; moreover, they despise it. One rap-aficionado I interviewed said he'd 'rather cut [his] balls off' than wear Picaldi. Another, who owns an urban/streetwear store, immediately started talking about 'Stone-Age people' and said that since he's been selling to people like that he avoids his own store's sales floor and basically hides away in his office. People regularly roll their eyes or laugh uncomfortably when the brand name is mentioned. There are nightclubs with 'No Picaldi' signs on their door. A sales clerk told me of a school in which Picaldi clothing was not allowed (though I have not been able to verify this). Searching for Picaldi on social networking sites such as Studi-VZ, Myspace or Facebook, one finds fan-page groups and groups with titles such as 'Thanks to Picaldi, I am able to immediately spot idiots.'

Such a list of impressions could be expanded and transformed into an entire phenomenology of dislike, contempt and disgust – both in the multiethnic western and in the predominantly 'German' eastern part of the city. Moreover, it indicates a basic fact of contemporary culture: despite undeniable tendencies toward a pluralization of identities that can be 'recognized' and seen as 'legitimate', in youth culture, too, there are basic ethnic and class divides that underpin cultural identities. A crucial concept in the language of disgust and contempt is *peinlich* which translates as 'embarrassing'. In the attitudes that many (basically, but not exclusively, middle- and upper-class) people hold toward Picaldi and its customers – and this concerns different forms of dislike – *projected embarrassment* is an important characteristic. Especially in teenage culture, a person, and not only a situation, can be seen as *peinlich,* 'embarrassing' in that sense. Why, though, would those jeans and the style they belong to be thought of as *embarrassing* in the first place? There certainly are people who feel shame, embarrassment, or humiliation in specific situations, and more widely as well, because they are wearing Picaldi clothing and others disapprove of that. The crucial point here, however, is that some people think, or viscerally sense, that others *should* be embarrassed. Used in that sense, the adjective *peinlich* (embarrassing) refers to an ascription of shame. Of course, the relevance of such 'demands' would be diminished if 'communities' autonomously set their own standards, social relations were experienced as straightforwardly antagonistic, or pluralistic cultural democracy had arrived. Indeed, obviously, most of Picaldi's customers most likely do not feel embarrassed at all. They may not be consciously aware of such dislikes, or they may not care. Lacking an awareness of or regard for other people's judgment is a basic characteristic of the type of assertiveness under consideration here, after all. Popular culture lends discursive frameworks to such sentiments of disregard. In his song 'Sonnenbank Flavour', for instance, Bushido lists various aspects of both 'street' toughness and lifestyle practices, and he describes himself as 'being on the *Proll-track*' (*Proll-Schiene*). In doing so, he articulates a self-confident identification with a much-ridiculed cultural figure. These kinds of value charge reversals and re-significations are, of course, common throughout histories of popular culture, and they play a role in this cultural field as well. In this case, however, the reversal isn't complete or sustainable, as despite such examples, the epithet so far has not turned into an unproblematic term of self-ascription.[19]

Male physicality and sexual attractiveness are crucial to the issue of projected embarrassment as well. With regard to the carrot-cut jeans, such questions are alluded to, for instance, in press reports about Picaldi, where customers are referred to as 'macho bodies' or a prototypical 'prole who stages his physicalness without so much as a hint of self-consciousness'.[20] The most widely circulated text about Picaldi appeared in the major weekly *Der Stern* under the headline 'Auf dicke Hose', which refers to the idiom 'einen auf dicke Hose machen' which has the idiomatic meaning of showing off, playing it big – monetarily, but with sexual undertones. With its high-waist fit and overall body schema, the Diesel/Picaldi carrot-cut, 'figurbetont' (figure-highlighting) as it is, seems like a breach of decorum, a 'flaunted', vulgar, unsophisticated form of male sexual display, which contrasts with bourgeois restraint and modesty, but also with various varieties of alternative masculinities and, importantly, with the 'metrosexual' mode of male sexualization in popular culture of more recent years (cf. Gill 2005; Richard 2005). An article in a city weekly magazine about working-class youth, for instance, mentioned 'a fashion that seems to communicate something. Some call it sexual aggressiveness.'[21] Of course, such sources are hardly unproblematic, yet they do seem to make explicit an important subtext: in designating this physicality as embarrassing, I think it is fair to assume that people cannot help but implicitly relate to their *own* physicality, desires, and inhibitions, however important that may or may not be in the individual instance. Furthermore, the notion of embarrassment generally refers to a form of failure, an inability to successfully perform something one sets out (or is set up) to do in the eyes of others. Here, however, people seem to be attacking both *presumption,* such as when they ridicule the apparent strivings of prepubescent boys, who just aren't who they are apparently pretending to be (in all sorts of ways, including sexual), and that which they are striving *toward.* In some ways, such dismissal and ridicule would hardly be socially acceptable among many of its proponents were it not articulated primarily on the class level.

In focusing – in a highly condensed form – on outside views as well as inside views, I have not meant to suggest that the former are what matter most about Picaldi denim. I do suggest, however, that the figurations of inside and outside perspectives elucidate sociocultural dynamics that would otherwise not be visible. Among the many aspects that characterize the experience of wearing these specific jeans as part of an overall style, the embodied attitude of assertiveness – swagger – plays an important role, as I have shown, which is often connected to an empowering sense of ambiguity in self-presentation (with regard to risky behaviour). Is he a good boy? And if so, then in what sense? In the outside view, however, much of that is decoded not in terms of ambiguity but as failure and presumption on the one hand, and a threat on the other. Such an attitude manifests in projected embarrassment, among other sentiments and interaction patterns. These, then, are the 'local genres of anxiety' which congeal in emblematic types of denim and its uses.

The Right to Ambiguity

In literary terms, the underlying structure of what I have described and analysed has a *tragic* character in that cultural processes on the experiential level help cement and affectively legitimize social relations and position ascriptions that the actors might not support explicitly. Again, this is not to suggest that these processes are what ultimately determines social structures (or even experiences) but they do represent one medium for living through them, and, potentially, challenging them. It is important to also note some fault lines within such processes. Here, the explicitly normative domain is particularly relevant, outside the directly political realm as well. In talking about clothing, perception and stereotypes, many who sport the carrot-cut, and the 'gangsta style' more generally, do not just present themselves ambiguously in regard to toughness. In talking about it (and, I would argue, in practice), they also lay claims to a *right to ambiguity*. The claim can be summed up by a formulaic statement of this kind:

> Yes, I wear stuff that makes me look tough. No, I don't mind that people may take me for a thug. I can see why they would feel intimidated, and I kind of like that. At the same time, these are just clothes. I deserve to be treated like everybody else. Clothes don't tell the story of an individual. No one should be categorized on such superficial terms.

There are many such stories, and they may sound familiar. Often straightforward ethnic discrimination dominates them, but it is rationalized in terms of clothing. 'Everybody' knows, for instance, that getting into a nightclub wearing Picaldi (the jackets and sweater rather than the jeans) and Picaldi-style overall is hard (even though there are exceptions, especially for 'Germans'), and many think that this is unfair. Tayfun, for instance, talks about older people regularly changing the side of the street when they see him approach. He is genuinely disturbed by their perceptions of him – even though, he says, his 'boxer haircut' is moderate, and he is merely wearing what he likes, just like other young people do, but different rules seem to apply to him. Another such story comes from a young man named Marco, a 'white German' from a middle-class family, who is into the overall Picaldi style. He recalls getting into a long discussion with a girl he found attractive, after he had approached her on the street and she completely ignored his advances. She basically fit the general type of an 'alternative' style. These people, he says (somewhat frustrated after what appear to have been a number of similar rejections), are the most prejudiced of all, because they will dismiss people like him – as a 'Proll' – on the mere basis of clothing.

The critical and reflective mode in which such claims and observations are formulated doesn't seem to square easily with the assertiveness, dominance, and insistence on invulnerability that characterizes the discursive and physical figure that is under consideration here. Indeed, while some talk in that way, many others would not engage in this type of discourse, at least not toward me (and probably not in other situations either). The point is that in claiming something like a right to ambiguity, a rights-granting entity is addressed as a potential interlocutor in a process of recognition. In the context of a stylized, avowedly antagonistic attitude, such recourse is anything but obvious. On the one hand, this fact simply confirms that, in many instances, antagonism is a pose. On the other hand, there also is a profound resonance between such claims and the core structure of the cultural formats that pervade those discourses. This resonance can be illustrated by returning to the similarities between Tarek's practice of impression management and the question of what is 'real' in gangsta rap where, as I showed, the plane of lyrical content contrasts with its being formally framed as aesthetics for which, in our societies, different rules apply. The potential de-escalation of semantic content through discursive recourse to (aesthetic) form or frame is even more apparent in the domain of clothing, where, quite obviously, people are generally willing and able to distinguish between statements made by wearing clothes, and statements in a literal sense. The former can or cannot be taken seriously, and people who do so in a way deemed inappropriate may be ridiculed as lacking an acute enough sense of reality. Furthermore, the physical, affective and social dimensions of clothing, their experiential texture, as it were, do not primarily have a predicative structure, just as the musical texture makes it inappropriate and unfair for rap music to be reduced to its lyrical content – experientially as well as on the level of discursive explication. By wearing, for instance, specific denim, then, one makes statements, in a somewhat conscious manner, but one reserves the right to change frames of meaning: from assertion to ambiguity, from the serious to the playful. Of course, the problematic isn't always explicitly elaborated in terms of such a claim. Its efficacy can only be approximated by comparing it to a rule or to discursive statements. Rather, ambiguity of this type can be felt, performed, lived – it is, in a way, a 'structure of feeling' and its verbal expression is embedded in various practices.

Notes

1   The term 'subculture', as it was refashioned by the Birmingham school of Cultural Studies in the 1970s (cf. Clarke et al. 1976), has come under much criticism since the mid-1990s (cf. Muggleton and Weinzierl 2003), but cases such as this one show its continuing relevance, if only as a pointer toward the articulation of homologies through complex, multi-scale cultural practices, within contexts in which specific social determinants play a significant role. For a view close to my own cf. Hesmondhalgh (2005).

2   In this chapter I remain agnostic toward the important and politically charged debates over analytical terminology, both in regard to processual terms such as exclusion (Bude 2006, 2008a, 2008b; Knecht 1999; Kronauer 2002) and analytical group designations such as working-class (Skeggs 2004), precariat (in the wake of Bourdieu 1998), multitude (Virno 2004), *Unterschicht* in the sense of popular classes

(Warneken 2006) or of an 'underclass' (Nolte 2004; cf., for instance, the critique in Lindner and Musner 2008).

3   In this piece, there is little space for theoretical and methodological considerations. My analysis focuses on a 'plane of experience', which incorporates various types of phenomena (or analytical registers), such as sentiments, affects, discourses, structures of interaction and cultural dynamics.

4   And those by some other local brands that have followed this example in recent years, carrying similar faux-Italian brand names, Daggio Romanzo, Blucino and Casa.

5   Through two companies, the owner of Unplugged and his partners import and wholesale the products of the Turkish company Picaldi in Germany (and Austria). Furthermore, much or even most of the design process of the articles sold in Germany takes place here as well, although this has been going back and forth in regard to the 'basics' among the jeans.

6   Such classifications are not only highly problematic, their meanings, borders and their relevance are part of what gets negotiated and 'performed' in such processes. Ethnic classifications with reference to 'migration background', to a category such as whiteness, to nationality and citizenship are only seemingly obvious. All of them, in specific ways, are social constructions and selections that are, however, not random, but rely on a number of persistent institutions and ideologies. The most obvious example is that many 'foreigners' are in fact Germans but not recognized or accepted as such by others, in large part because of ethnic *(völkisch)* understandings of citizenship.

7   As did the album 'Hart(z) IV' by rapper Eko Fresh, in which he was pictured wearing a Picaldi sweater. Hart translates as 'tough', Hartz is the last name of a former Volkswagen manager who famously consulted the federal government in the process of social safety-net 'reforms' and gave his name to various phases of these reforms, including 'Hartz IV', which largely abolished the distinction between longer term unemployment benefits and welfare (Arbeitslosengeld II).

8   The carrot-cut has, for a long time, been much more popular for women's jeans, but that seems to be an entirely different story.

9   On men's jeans as 'adding body' – see Sassatelli (2011). Sassatelli's research is based on data collected in Milan, Italy.

10   In: *Spex* Nr. 313, 3/4, 2008.

11   The jeans are just one – though especially relevant – element or this style (which can largely be understood as a subcultural style), a basic standard, which people combine with other, sometimes more conspicuous and expensive items.

12   What is 'authentic' is determined by cultural evaluations, not by mere facts in the world (Lindner 2001), and it represents an especially difficult notion within racialized contexts.

13   The pejorative use of *schwul* (gay) is common in that scene. While it shouldn't be taken as a literal insult, and falling into immediate outrage might just play into the communicative strategy, it certainly remains an objectionable form of homophobia that powerfully reinforces latent forms thereof, and indicates an orientation on specific, unambiguous forms of masculinity and a rejection of what is considered effeminateness. In order to retain some semblance of adequateness to musical differentiations, it should be noted that Kool Savas, for instance, isn't a gangsta rapper but is famous for his lyrical skill in freestyle 'battle' and his vulgar lyrics.

14   'Keinen Arsch in der Hose haben', not having an ass in one's pants, means lacking courage or assertiveness.

15   'Alpha-Jacke': pilot jackets by the Texas-based company Alpha Industries.

16   'Einen auf X machen' basically means to play X, to act as if one was X.

17   Such metaphors include *einen Film schieben* or *in einem Film sein* '(literally 'being in a film'), or composites of *Schiene* 'rail'.

18 It seems plausible to assume that this type of feeling is nothing new at all (cf. Pearson 1983). Further-more, similar mechanisms of medialization through figures have been at play for at least decades, especially since the 'amplification' of subcultural deviance and violence (think mods versus teds, skins) in the 1950s and 1960s. Cf. the primarily British literature on subcultures, amplification and 'moral panics' (Cohen 1973).

19 Within the context of rap-oriented scene, for instance, people are more likely to adapt terms such as 'Kanake' [sic], 'Gangster' and 'Atze' than 'Proll'. This is reminiscent of what Hartigan (2005) has written about 'white trash' – despite some resignification, the term largely remained 'socially un-inhabitable'.

20 *DeutschlandRadio,* 'Picaldi und Konsorten – Mode unter Migrantenkids in Berlin', 9 April 2003. It should be noted that, in the radio report, this quote is used critically in summarizing a view that some people (whose prejudices the report is critical of) seem to hold.

21 *Zitty* 8/2005, p. 21.

References

Androutsopoulos, Jannis. 'Musiknetzwerke. Identitätsarbeit auf HipHopWebsites.' In *Coolhunters. Jugendkulturen zwischen Medien und Markt*, edited by Klaus Neumann-Braun and Birgit Richard. Frankfurt am Main: Suhrkamp, 2005: 159–72.

Bourdieu, Pierre. *Distinction. A Social Critique of the Judgement of Taste.* Cambridge, MA: Harvard University Press, 1984.

Bourdieu, Pierre. 'Prekarität ist überall.' In *Gegenfeuer. Wortmeldungen im Dienste des Widerstands gegen die neoliberale Invasion,* edited by Pierre Bourdieu. Konstanz: UVK, 1998: 96–102.

Bude, Heinz, ed. *Das Problem der Exklusion. Ausgegrenzte, Entbehrliche, Überflüssige.* Hamburg: Hamburger Edition, 2006.

Bude, Heinz. *Die Ausgeschlossenen. Das Ende vom Traum einer gerechten Gesellschaft.* München: Hanser, 2008a.

Bude, Heinz and Andreas Willisch, eds. *Exklusion. Die Debatte über die 'Überflüssigen'.* Frankfurt am Main: Suhrkamp, 2008b.

Clarke, John, Stuart Hall, Tony Jefferson and Brian Roberts. 'Subcultures, Cultures and Class.' In *Resistance Through Rituals: Youth Subcultures in Post-War Britain*, edited by Stuart Hall and Tony Jefferson. London: Hutchinson, 1976.

Cohen, Stanley. *Folk Devils and Moral Panics. The Creation of the Mods and Rockers.* St Albans: Paladin, 1973.

Duden. Das große Wörterbuch der deutschen Sprache in zehn Bänden. 3., völlig überarbeitete und erweiterte Auflage. Wissenschaftlicher Rat der Dudenredaktion. Vol. 7: Pekt-Schi. Mannheim: Dudenverlag, 1999.

Gill, Rosalind, Karen Henwood and Carl McLean. 'Body Projects and the Regulation of Normative Masculinity.' In *Body and Society* 2005, 11: 37–62.

Goffman, Erving. *The Presentation of Self in Everyday Life.* Garden City, NY: Doubleday, 1959.

Hardt, Michael. 'Foreword: What Affects Are Good For.' In *The Affective Turn. Theorizing the Social*, edited by Patricia Ticineto Clough and Jean Halley. Durham, NC: Duke University Press, 2007: ix–xiii.

Hartigan, John Jr. *Odd Tribes. Toward A Cultural Analysis of White People.* Durham, NC: Duke University Press, 2005.

Hesmondhalgh, David. 'Subcultures, Scenes or Tribes? None of the Above.' In *Journal of Youth Studies* 8(1)2005: 21–40.

Knecht, Michi, ed. *Armut und Ausgrenzung in Berlin*. Köln: Böhlau, 1999: 7–25.

Kronauer, Martin. *Exklusion. Die Gefährdung des Sozialen im hochentwickelten Kapitalismus*. Frankfurt am Main/New York: Campus, 2002.

Lahire, Bernard. *L'homme pluriel. Les ressorts de l'action*. Paris: Hachette, 2001.

Lindner, Rolf. 'The Construction of Authenticity: The Case of Subcultures.' In *Locating Cultural Creativity*, edited by John Liep. London: Pluto, 2001.

Lindner, Rolf and Lutz Musner, eds. *Unterschicht. Kulturwissenschaftliche Erkundungen der 'Armen' in Geschichte und Gegenwart*. Freiburg: Rombach, 2008.

Massumi, Brian. 'Requiem for Our Prospective Dead (Toward a Participatory Critique of Capitalist Power).' In *Deleuze and Guattari. New Mappings in Politics, Philosophy and Culture*, edited by Eleanor Kaufman and Kevin J. Heller. London/Minneapolis, MN: University of Minnesota Press, 1998: 40–64.

Miller, Daniel and Sophie Woodward. 'Manifesto for a Study of Denim.' In *Social Anthropology/Anthropologie Sociale* 15(3)2007: 335–51.

Moore, Anne E. *Unmarketable. Brandalism, Copyfighting, Mocketing, and the Erosion of Integrity*. New York: New Press, 2007.

Muggleton, David and Rupert Weinzierl, eds. *The Post-Subcultures Reader*. Oxford: Berg, 2003.

Neckel, Sighard. 'Kampf um Zugehörigkeit. Die Macht der Klassifikation.' In *Leviathan* 31(2)2003: 159–67.

Nolte, Paul. *Generation Reform. Jenseits der blockierten Republik*. München: Beck, 2004.

Pearson, Geoffrey. *Hooligan. A History of Respectable Fears*. Basingstoke: Macmillan, 1983.

Richard, Birgit. 'Beckham's Style Kicks! Die meterosexuellen Körperbilder der Jugendidole.' In *Coolhunters*, edited by Neumann-Braun and Richard: 244–60.

Sayer, Andrew. *The Moral Significance of Class*. Cambridge: Cambridge University Press, 2006.

Sassatelli, Roberta. "Indigo Bodies: Fashion, Mirror Work and Sexual Identity in Milan." In *Global Denim,* edited by Daniel Miller and Sophie Woodward. Oxford et al.: Berg, 2011.

Skeggs, Beverly. *Class, Self, Culture*. London: Routledge, 2004.

Tyler, Imogen. 'Chav Mum Chav Scum.' In *Feminist Media Studies* 8(1)2008: 17–34.

Sutterlüty, Ferdinand and Ina Walter. 'Übernahmegerüchte. Klassifikationskämpfe zwischen türkischen Aufsteigern und ihren deutschen Nachbarn.' In *Leviathan* 33(2)2005: 182–204.

Virno, Paolo. *A Grammar of the Multitude: For an Analysis of Contemporary Forms of Life*. Los Angeles: Semiotext(e), 2004.

Warneken, Bernd Jürgen. *Die Ethnographie popularer Kulturen. Eine Einführung*. Köln: Böhlau, 2006.

NELE BRÖNNER

Anthropology of the City

Rolf Lindner

The Imaginary of the City

Pour distinguer sérieusement deux lieux réels,
ne faut-il pas d'abord chercher ce que les distingue imaginairement?

Sansot 1971: 22

In recent years the imaginary of the city has become a subject of anthropology. The fact that this occurred above all in France is undoubtedly related to the French tradition of addressing questions of "mentalité" and "mémoire collective". Seen phenomenologically, this research is a response to the familiar conditions of media superimposition on and penetration of urban space, but one which does not lapse into fashionable talk of the "unreality" of cities. One could, on the contrary, say that the accompanying pictures and symbols make the physical space even more "real", since the imaginary is not, after all, opposed to reality, but draws on it and "deepens" it is a specific way: "Nous pretendrons que le vécu nourrit, anthentifie certaines mythologies (celles des journeaux, des rengaines, des romans faciles) et que celles-ci, en revanche, donnent consistance au vécu (les paroles, les marches, les habitudes des hommes de la ville)" (Sansot 1971: 18). Hence what is meant by superimposition on and penetration of urban space making it unrecognisable, but rather renders it hyper-recognisable: "cet imaginaire donne un sens au lieu, un 'supplement d'âme qui nous interpelle" (Cherubini 1995: 80). It is this surplus which makes of the city not only a lived place, but also a dreamed one, as the French historian Arlette Farge (1995) has put it. The Imaginary of the city, in Pierre Sansot's poetic formulation, is "la reverie du réel", the Fantasy of the real.

In taking up the "Imaginary of the city" as a theme, anthropology is returning to a neglected sociological approach, that of "cultural representation", which Richard Wohl and Anselm Strauss introduced in 1958 in their essay "Symbolic Representation and the Urban Milieu". "If, as Robert Park suggested, the city is a state of mind, then people must respond psychologically to their urban environment; they must, to some extent, attempt to grasp the meaning of its complexity imaginatively and symbolically as well as literally" (Wohl and Strauss 1958: 523). Wohl and Strauss were the first to raise the question of the meaning of the city for its inhabitants, of its evocative and expressive qualities. It is certainly an ironic comment on our supposedly post-local age with its nomadic lifestyles, that in Pulp Fiction, a work celebrated as a small masterpiece of postmodern film, the reference to the place of origin of one of its heroes (Cass from Inglewood) is enough to vividly convey a whole character. Origins still matter, and sometimes in a painful way. Wohl and Strauss regarded the characterisation of cities by an "indigenous symbolism" as necessary, so that their inhabitants can digest, connect and fit in the wealth of impressions and experiences to which they are permanently exposed. It is not only the symbols, which stand for the whole, which serve to express the essence of urban experience, the "Wahrzeichen" as the typical German notion has it, the landmarks and emblems such as the skyline of New York, which is so well understood as a symbol, "that a movie can establish its locale by doing no more than flashing a picture of these skyscrapers on the screen for a moment and then directing the camera into the opening episodes of the film" (Wohl and Strauss 1958: 526), but also a "vocabulary", from the allegory to the analogy, from the anecdote to the popular song, from the urban legends to the poem, which helps citizens to formulate the uniqueness of their city in comparison and in contrast to the other towns.

To show that in the course of time texts accumulate in this way, that these texts form a texture in which the city is truly enmeshed, has been the contribution of Gerald D. Suttles, one of the few urban researchers to pursue the symbolic-representational approach of Wohl and Strauss. In an essay with the programmatic title "The Cumulative Texture of Local Urban Culture" (1984), Suttles rejects an urban sociology which regards city life exclusively in terms of the economic endpoints of production and consumption and sees local culture merely as the cause of minor deviations, an element in economic retardation or simply a set of exogenous factors. The biography of a city cannot be adequately understood if reliance is placed exclusively on economic explanatory models; to achieve a "thick description" or the specificity of a city it is necessary to take into account the cumulative texture of the local culture as expressed in images, typifications and collective representations. What makes Suttles' essay a seminal text, even today, is less that it points to a research deficit (which is by now somewhat banal), but rather the wealth of material, which he recommends to the researcher's attention (from cemeteries to telephone books), and the specific logic by which, in his view, the pattern is woven into the fabric. Research will in his opinion usually yield three interrelated series of collective representations: first the founding or discovering figures of the place; second the economic and political elites, who "by hook or crook", have contributed to its "Spirit"; and thirdly artefacts of a material (such as monuments) and immaterial kind (such as sayings, songs and stories, which express the "Character" of the place) (Suttles 1984: 288). Though there might be a certain US-American bias in the choice of important items, the list gives us nonetheless an idea of what we can look for. Suttles sees these representations as directly linked to a distinct economic regime. In his examples these are the merchant families of Boston, the financial empires of New York, the joint-stock companies of Chicago, the "dream factories" of Los Angeles, and the oil companies and space exploration enterprises of Houston. This relationship is particularly clear in popular "characterology": "Proper Bostonian", "New York's city slicker", "Chicago's hog butchers", "Los Angeles' stars" and "Houston's wildcatters" (Suttles 1984: 291). In her recent study on Invented Cities Mona Domosh has shown how the built forms of New York and Boston differed according to what we might call the "ethos" of the respective elite classes, an ethos which is "frozen" in the popular stereotypes mentioned above. Urban landscapes are created within specific economic and social contexts that give them shape and meaning so that the landscapes become visible representations of group beliefs, values, tensions, and fears: "If New York was the quintessential bourgeois society, then the social scene in Boston in the late nineteenth century was characterised by its urban gentry" (Domosh 1996: 2). By interpreting the respective urban landscapes, on the one hand, as self-representative expression of the status aspiration of the bourgeois, on the other as the "good taste" of the urban gentry, Domosh confirms in her way the image of the "proper Bostonian" versus "New York's slicker". For Suttles local cultural representations display a remarkable durability. Their number certainly increases over time, but they do not fundamentally change. That is what is meant by the cumulative nature of local culture. Writers and/or literary genres play an essential part in the development and consolidation of the image of a particular city. There are cities which resemble a penny novel, whereas others are more likely to call a classics edition to mind. Some cities remind one of science fiction, whereas others make one think of sentimental rural narratives.

Cities have their authors just as authors have their cities: Raymond Chandler seems only to be conceivable in Los Angeles, Nelson Algren only in Chicago, Tom Wolfe only in New York. Thus literary works which aim at a unity of place and plot appear to be especially interesting sources for an urban ethnography, as Suttles has demonstrated: "Boston may have its Sister Carries and Chicago its George Apleys, but they are implausible literary characters" (Suttles 1984: 292). Thus the plausibility of a literary figure is a fine indicator for what is imaginable and above all what is unimaginable with regard to a particularity. Nothing is more characteristic of a particular city than what is not evident, what is taken to be impossible, what seems to be unthinkable.

The image of a city "migrates" across genres of writing, as James Donald (1992: 457) has put it, and the 'texts' which both reflect and perpetuate the image of a city are manifold and diverse. They include not only literary works, but also TV series, films, pop music and comics, not forgetting the numerous "instructive texts" such as local newspapers, listing magazines, guide books, tourist leaflets, postcards, or grand narratives like local histories and commemorative publications of every kind. What must be kept in mind with respect to these texts is the "characterological unity of local cultural representations" (Suttles), which results from the many-voiced variation of a basic theme and leads to a stereotypical and firmly established image. Even "der Schmäh", the polemic, which seeks to break with this image, ends up by confirming it, demonstrating that the image is impossible to avoid. The basic theme, on which variations are played, is not an arbitrary one, but is produced by that sector of the economy which has dominated the city historically. Out of the literary translation of the dominant sector of the city of Chicago, for example, the stock yards, into "hog butcher", into the "butcher to the world", by way of correspondences of the most diverse kind (from the letters of Polish immigrants, which take over this image via Saul Bellow who calls Chicago in an interview "ruder, cruder, noisier, dirtier, grosser, wildly energetic", to the city's promotional campaigns, which flirt with being tough but honest – contrasting the "honest Chicago guy" with the "arrogant New York upstart"), is created that habitus which even today, a quarter of a century after the demolition of the stock yards, makes Chicago still appear "Stormy, husky, and brawling", as it says in Carl Sandburg's poem "Chicago" from 1915.

We are only at the beginning of an ethnographic reading of the cumulative texture of cities. Ulf Hannerz's (1993) anthropological sketches of Amsterdam are one starting point. Another example of an ethnographic reading of a city was recently presented by the Dutch anthropologist Henk Driessen (1995) in his analysis of "Transitional Tangier". That transitory character developed both out of the particular location of Tangier as a port at the crossroads of Europe and Africa, of Occident and Orient, of Atlantic Ocean and Mediterranean, and of the status of the city as an international zone from 1912 to 1956. This turned Tangier not only into a center of communication, a place where money and gold were traded, and a haven for wealthy exiles and illegal refugees, but also into a screen on which fantasies were projected (with the B movie and the penny novel as characteristic media) and which attracted marginal characters of every kind. *The City of Quartz* seems to be the first full-blown study of the cumulative textures. Mike Davis (1990) investigated among other things, the role successive generations of intellectuals have played in the construction and deconstruction of the mythography of Los Angeles, the "world capital of the cultural industries". The cornerstone of the cultural productivity which became a material force in the development of the city were the literary invention of Southern California as a Mediterranean-like idyll of Hispanic culture by the so-called "Arroyo-Circle" (which became the script of the huge real estate speculations of the turn of the century), and the anti-myth of noir from Chandler to Cain and up to Polanski's *Chinatown,* a film which tells the history of L.A. as a history of speculation, corruption and crime (based on real estate capital as the dominant economic sector of the city) and so interweaves myth and anti-myth in complex fashion. Polanski and Davis are, in fact, very similar in this respect, as are, as a very recent example, James Ellroy/Curtis Hanson *(L.A. Confidential)* and Davis, both presenting L.A. as a melange of sunshine and noir. Thus the best representation of the cumulative textures so far weaves a new thread in the tissue of the imaginary of the city.

References

Cherubini, Bernard. "L'ambiance urbaine: un défi pour l'ecriture ethnographique." In *Journal des anthropologues* no. 61/62, 1995: 79–87.
Davis, Mike. *City of Quartz. Excavating the Future in Los Angeles.* London, New York: Verso, 1990.
Domosh, Mona. *Invented Cities. The Creation of Landscape in Nineteenth Century New York and Boston.* New Haven, London: Yale University Press, 1996.

Donald, James. "Metropolis: The City as Text." In *Social and Cultural Forms of Modernity*, edited by Robert Bocock and Kenneth Thompson. Cambridge, Oxford: Polity Press, 1992: 417–461.

Driessen, Henk. "Transitional Tangier. Some Notes on Passage and Representation." In *Kea. Zeitschrift für Kulturwissenschaften* 8, 1995: 149–161.

Farge, Arlette. "Ville derobée et subie, ville inventée XVIIIéme siécle." In *Journal des anthropologues* no. 61/62, 1995: 89–95.

Hannerz, Ulf. "Thinking about culture in cities." In *Understanding Amsterdam*, edited by Leon Deben, Willem Heinemeijer and Dick van der Vaart. Amsterdam (1993) 2000: 141–178.

Hannerz, Ulf. "Cities as windows on the world." In *Understanding Amsterdam*, edited by Deben, Heinemeijer and van der Vaart. Amsterdam, (1993) 2000: 179–196.

Sansot, Pierre. *Poétique de la ville*. Paris: Klincksieck, 1971.

Suttles, Gerald D. "The Cumulative Texture of Local Urban Culture." In *American Journal of Sociology* Vol. 90, 1984: 283–304.

Wohl, Richard R. and Anselm Strauss. "Symbolic Representation and the Urban Milieu." In *American Journal of Sociology* Vol. 63, 1958: 523–532 .

NELE BRÖNNER

Jonathan Raban

The City as Melodrama

What did these vain and presumptuous men intend?
How did they expect to raise this lofty mass against God,
when they had built it above all the mountains and clouds of the earth's atmosphere?

Saint Augustine on Babylon, *City of God,* Bk XV

The city has always been an embodiment of hope and a source of festering guilt: a dream pursued, and found vain, wanting, and destructive. Our current mood of revulsion against Cities is not new; we have grown used to looking for Utopia only to discover that we have created Hell. We are accustomed to gazing at America to make out our future, and in America the city is widely regarded as the sack of excrement which the country has to carry on its back to atone for its sins. Radio, television, magazines, colleges mount ritual talk-ins in which the word 'urban', pronounced in the hushed and contrite tone of a *mea culpa,* is monotonously followed by the two predicates, 'problems' and 'renewal'. On these joyless occasions, it is made clear that the problems have no real solutions, and that the notion of rehabilitation is a piece of empty piety, a necessary fiction in which no one really believes. When Mayor Lindsay of New York made his abortive bid for the Democratic Presidential nomination in 1972, the only tangible result of his campaign was a flood of sick jokes about the garbage in his streets, animal, vegetable, and mineral. It further became apparent that nobody in the United States wanted a big-city president: better to look to Maine, Alabama, South Dakota, California, whose native sons would not be polluted by the stench of those cities where most of America's domestic troubles are located.

A middle-sized American city at 7 p.m., after the commuters have taken to their cars and the too-bright sodium lights show through the quickening dusk (I am thinking of Worcester, Hartford, Springfield Mass.), feels like a burnt-out dream. No one is about, bar a dusting of blacks, Puerto Ricans, Chicanos, and they have the furtive air of people habituated to being always suspected of being up to something. The white-domed Statehouse, memorial of a grandiose colonial conception of civic order, looks a tartarous yellow. A hundred years ago, people put up portly brownstone houses along wide wooded avenues. Their architecture is proud, but one can almost smell the rot in the stone, rank and soggy with inattention. In the hallways, you catch a whiff of bacon-fat and Lysol. Each apartment door has a winking spyhole cut into the wood, and people live behind chains and double-locks, with mail-order .38 revolvers tucked handily into a drawer along with the napery. The humans most in evidence are the policemen. Their car headlights rake housefronts for junkies, and you can hear their klaxons screaming, always a block or two away, like invisibly ominous owls. After midnight, in the neon-blaze of the Dunkin' Donuts shop you can see them, a line of broad bums stretched over red plastic stools, their pistols hanging out on straps like monstrous genital accessories.

Or there is the dismal story of Bixby Hill on the outskirts of Los Angeles. There nice people have erected their $150,000 homes inside a fortified stockade, eight feet high, patrolled by heavily armed security guards, with an electronic communication system installed in every house. In a TV programme about this armourplated ghetto, a shrill housewife, surrounded by hardware and alarm-buttons, said, 'We are trying to preserve values and morals here that are decaying on the outside.' And her husband, a comfortable Babbitty figure, told the reporter: 'When I pass by the guard in the evening, I'm safe, I'm home, it's just a lovely feeling, it really is.' When they talked of the city beyond the walls, they conjured a vision of Gomorrah where the respectable and the innocent are clubbed, butchered, burglarised, where every patch of shadow has its resident badman with a knife, a gleam in his eye, and a line of punctures up his forearm.

Perhaps the original dream of the American city, with its plazas, squares, avenues, and Washingtonian circles, was too optimistic and elevated for reality. On Chestnut Street and Elm Street, the trees languished. But the present disreputable state of *civitas* in the United States is the product of an exaggeratedly Calvinist sense of sin. Finding the city irredeemable is only the other side of the coin to expecting it to be Paradise: utopias and dystopias go, of necessity, hand in hand. Disillusion is a vital part of the process of dreaming – and may, one suspects, prove almost as enjoyable. When New Yorkers tell one about the dangers of their city, the muggings, the dinner parties to which no one turns up for fear of being attacked on the way, the traffic snarl-ups, the bland indifference of the city cops, they are unmistakably bragging. Living in Greenwich Village is almost as exciting as war-service, and beneath the veneer of concerned moralism it is not hard to detect a vein of scoutlike enthusiasm for adventure. The New Yorker, echoing Whitman, is a proud participant in the decadence which has made his city even more world-famous than it was before: he is the man, he suffers, he is there.

His nightmare city is simply an ideal city in reverse, just as the great ideal cities in history, from Plato's Republic to Le Corbusier's Radiant City, have been constructed in protest against the uninspiring conditions of cities as they actually were and are. The failures and imperfections of Athens, Rome, London, New York, Paris have given rise to towns in books which in their architecture, their social and political life, would express man's highest aspirations to perfectibility. The very existence of the city, with its peculiar personal freedoms and possibilities, has acted as a licence for sermons and dreams. Here society might be arranged for man's greatest good; here, all too often, it has seemed a sink of vice and failure. Nor has this melodramatic moralistic view of city life been the exclusive province of philosophers and theologians; political bosses, architects, town planners, even those professionally tweedy sceptics, sociologists, have happily connived at the idea of the city as a controllable option between heaven and hell. Bits and pieces of ideal cities have been incorporated into real ones; traffic projects and rehousing schemes are habitually introduced by their sponsors as at least preliminary steps to paradise. The ideal city gives us the authority to castigate the real one; while the sore itch of real cities goads us into creating ideal ones.

Saint Augustine wrote *The City of God* in a state of sorrowful contemplation of a succession of earthly cities. A modern ecologist looking at the effects of megalopolis could hardly have more cause for despair than Augustine staring at the mark of Cain on every city in history. Babylon, Troy, Athens, Rome, Syracuse had all fallen; Carthage itself was sacked on the morning of Augustine's death. There was a good reason for Cain, the first murderer, to found the first city. Ancient cities were, before all else, fortifications against hostile strangers; their architecture, like that of Bixby Hill, began not with the life of the community inside the walls but with defence against the marauders outside. So slaughter, pestilence, siege, sacking, plunder, and burning – to use Augustine's own words – were the city's inevitable fate. If, by some accident, the city survived sacking by foreigners, there were many precedents for the citizens to occasion their own ruin by shiftless self-indulgence. Byzantium failed to maintain its huge population (at its height, it had 500,000 inhabitants). There are desolate accounts of sheep grazing within the city walls, nibbling among the stumps of deserted dwellings. The medieval city, under constant threat of under-population, feared paganism and homosexuality for practical as well as moral reasons. The Christian cult of the family was the cornerstone of the expanding and prosperous city.

The economics of city life have always enabled an entertainment-industry to take root in a large town. The citizen has more money and more leisure than his country cousin, more opportunities to spoil himself at the circus, the theatre, the whorehouse. Augustine, grimly observing these antics, addressed himself to the crowd as they swarmed into the 'scenic games, exhibitions of folly and licence':

> Oh infatuated man, what is this blindness, or rather madness, which possesses you? How is it that while, as we hear, even the eastern nations are bewailing your ruin, and while powerful states in the most remote parts of the earth are mourning your fall as a public calamity, ye yourselves should be crowding to the theatres, should be pouring into them and filling them, and, in short, be playing a madder part now than ever before? This was the foul plague-spot, this the wreck of virtue and honour that Scipio sought to preserve you from when he prohibited the construction of theatres; this was his reason for desiring that you might still have an enemy to fear, seeing as he did how easily prosperity would corrupt and destroy you. He did not consider that republic flourishing whose walls stand, but whose morals are in ruins.

It is the very success of the city as an economic unit which causes its downfall as a spiritual republic, and that paradox is the hardest of all truths for Augustine to bear. The city of man ought to be a harmonious reflection of the city of God; in actuality, it is vulgar, lazy and corrupt, a place so brutish that it lacks even the dignity of the Satanic. Better the besieged city than the corpulent city, better poverty than wealth; for whatever nourishes the city chokes it too.

This is a diatribe that has gone soft with repeated use. William Cobbett saw London as 'the great Wen' and demanded that it be 'dismantled' in order that civilisation might have a second chance. William Booth wrote of it as 'The Slough of Despond'; for Jack London it was 'the abyss', for George Gissing, 'the nether world'. Behind all of these dystopian metaphors lies an anguished charge of disappointment, a sense of what the city might have been, *if only* … The theatres, strip-joints, brothels, slums, traffic jams are not simply bad in themselves; they are reminders that once we dreamed of something so much greater, a paradise on earth, and it has come to this. The man nearest in spirit to Saint Augustine today, Lewis Mumford, has devoted most of his life to a tireless explication of where we went wrong, how we might set it right. His histories, plans, critiques never falter from that vision of human perfectibility. In the idea of the new town, pioneered by Patrick Geddes and Ebenezer Howard, the real city was entirely abandoned to the corrupted troglodytes and all hope vested in what Howard called 'the garden cities of tomorrow'. They are with us today: Crawley and Welwyn, and they are hardly any nearer to Paradise than Wardour Street and Shaftesbury Avenue.

But Mumford, Geddes and Howard, though perhaps inspired by a measure of the same moral feeling as Saint Augustine, broke with him in one major and calamitous respect. They shifted the emphasis from the inner to the outer man, from the spiritual to the technical; Augustine's Vision of the twin cities of God and Man was wonderfully and delicately balanced; his writing exhibits a constant wonder at the sheer inventive fecundity of human civilisation, from the divine gift of reason to such obscure talents as that of the man who could fart in time to music. The tragedy of the secular city, as far as Augustine was concerned, was its failure to embody the good in man, its inherent susceptibility to the cruelty and violence of Cain. It was in the spirit of man, the capacity for good in the individual consciousness, that the salvation of the human city lay. But for Geddes and Mumford, the answer was to be found in techniques; and they coined a quasi-evolutionist vocabulary for technology … 'eotechnic', 'paleotechnic', 'neotechnic'. Individual reason and love had failed the city, so they resorted to a home-made stew of science, sociology, and bureaucratic administration. It was called, innocuously enough, town-planning; and it sought to revive the old dream of an ideal city, a Jerusalem the Golden, by means of faith, not in man himself, but in his structures.

They had some inauspicious precedents. Thomas Campanella was a Hermetic theologian and fashionable magus who was flung into prison and tortured by the Spanish Inquisition. In jail Campanella dreamed of a City of the Sun, whose nobility and enlightenment would shame the corrupt and fallen civics of Rome, Naples (where he spent his sentence), and Madrid. His *Civitas Solis* (1623) is lifeless: a representation of worthy hopes which is sadly innocent of imagination. But its broad outline is interesting, and both its aspirations and its failures of vision are not unconnected, I think, with those of much twentieth-century town-planning.

Campanella starts with architecture, and to begin with he shows us a city without people, or, at least, with only the wispiest of sketch-figures, of the kind that architects like to put (merely as indications of relative scale) walking outside projected factories and town halls. It consists of seven concentric fortified circles, named after the planets, and four streets following the points of the compass. At the centre is the Temple of Knowledge and Metaphysics, an awesome and uncomfortable place which sounds darkly like the Royal Festival Hall. Each of the seven city walls is painted with representations of various aspects of human knowledge – maths, geometry, botany, physics, folklore, geology, medicine, engineering, and so on – so that living in the city would be like inhabiting a symmetrical three-dimensional encyclopedia. Like the timid sculptures and murals which the Greater London Council dots about its prizewinning housing estates, these educational decorations were supposed to keep you in a continuous state of uplift and learning. It does not sound very joyful.

When Campanella eventually reaches the laws and customs of the citizens, he sketches the life of a puritanical, ecologically sound kibbutz. The community is run by observing the laws of nature and share-and-share alike. Prohibition is effective; speakeasies wouldn't have occurred to Campanella. Work means either agriculture or cottage craft-industries like weaving, ornament making, and carpentry. Gold and silver have no special value beyond their intrinsic prettiness. Women wear make-up and high-heeled shoes on pain of death.

It all has a drearily familiar ring to it. We need to be reminded that rural nostalgia is not by any means a post-nineteenth-century phenomenon. The trade economy of the city, with its merchants and entrepreneurs, its delegations of labour and responsibility, has always been created by those who dislike cities as an unnatural practice, a perversion of the 'natural' life of an agricultural economy. An 'ideal city' would live to the simple, seasonal rhythms of a rural village. But, as Jane Jacobs showed brilliantly in The Economy of Cities (1969), the myth of agricultural primacy has no foundation in either archaeology or economics. Cities do not necessarily grow out of the excess production of their pre-existing rural hinterlands; as often as not, it is the city which enables the spread of farming on its outskirts. Yet the myth has been used repeatedly to browbeat the city, and it is wielded with no more prescience by Lewis Mumford than it was by Campanella.

The City of the Sun, like so many ideal cities, wasn't a city at all. It lacked an urban social and economic structure, just as it lacked a genuinely urban architecture. The only thing which distinguished it from a village was its dogged high-mindedness, its air of being at two removes from real life. It was an anti-city; a reflection perhaps, of Campanella's resentment of cities as they were, as well as of a romantic innocence about the life of the country which he sought to use as a salve for the diseases of urban society. He was not so far from the architects and renewers of today; who love green space, rapid exit routes, convenience shopping areas which cut down on in-city movement and street life. They achieve a terrible parody of rural simplicity by bulldozing down the old, intricate structures and replacing them with massive slabs of pale concrete. Somewhere at the bottom of every planner's mind must be a dream like Campanella's: a dream of glass and grass and concrete, where a handful of watercolour humans, tapering from the shoulders down, flit their spidery way through an architecture so simple and gigantic that they cannot corrupt it.

So Le Corbusier laid down his fourteen cardinal principles in *La Ville Radieuse* (1935):

> The Plan: totalitarian
> The death of the street
> Classification of simple speeds and complex speeds
> Arrangements made to come to an agreement on imminent
> LAWS of machine civilisation, laws which can halt the menace
> of modern times
> The mobilisation of the soil, in both cities and rural areas
> Housing considered as an extension of the public services
> The green city
> The civilisation of the road replacing the civilisation of the railway
> Landscaping the countryside
> The radiant city
> The radiant country
> The twilight of money
> The essential joys, satisfaction of psycho-physiological
> needs, collective participation, and individual liberty
> The renaissance of the human body

This document deserves a close scrutiny, for it enshrines some of the most hallowed modern principles on which planners in London and New York are still acting to change our lives. It is both as conservative and as thinly idealistic as Campanella's totalitarian plan, as if the only thing which divided the twentieth century from the seventeenth was the invention of the motor car. Again the myth of agricultural primacy is presented as axiomatic: La Ville Radieuse is founded on 'the release of the soil' – courgettes and petits pois sprouting greenly between tower-blocks. There is the same undercurrent of hatred for the money economy of the city. The 'essential joys' are named and listed in such a way as to make us instantly wish not to have them. 'Les temps modernes' are linked to 'la menace' as surely as winter follows autumn, and architectural dictatorship, those grimly capitalised LAWS, must be immediately granted by society if the menace is to be fought off. As happens so often in the manifestoes of Modernism, what looks, at first sight, a brave and energetic release from slavery of old habits of thought, reveals itself to be in fact a shrilly puritanical backlash.

Corbusier clearly thought that the people were getting away with something, and must be stopped. His second principle, 'la mort de la rue', is the most radical and frightening of all. Take away the street, and one cuts out the heart of cities as they are actually used and lived in. Corbusier wanted a city of high-rise tower-blocks, and it is in that proposal that his profound conservatism is most evident. One can see why by looking at the very fair stab at a Radiant City which was made by Southampton City Council in the late nineteen-fifties and early 'sixties.

Four miles to the west of Southampton city centre, they built a housing estate called Millbrook, a vast, cheap storage unit for nearly 20,000 people. Laid out on a sloping plain, it has fifty acres of grassland at its centre, a great, useless, balding greenspace of sickly turf and purely symbolic value. What one sees first are the tower-blocks, twenty-four storeys high, of pre-stressed concrete and glass, known, I am told, as 'slab block/scissors-type', should anyone order more. The roads are service roads; they loop purposelessly around the estate in broad curves that conform to no contours. There is no street life on them: an occasional pram pushed by a windblown mother, a motorbiking yobbo or two, a dismal row of parked Ford Anglias, an ice-cream van playing 'Greensleeves' at half-tempo, a mongrel snapping at its tail. The acres of greensward sweep monotonously between the blocks, patrolled by gangs of sub-teenage youths and the occasional indecent-exposure freak. Church halls have been allocated by proportional representation, and a mathematical genius has worked out diametrical sites for the shopping plazas, with vandalised launderettes and 'Joyce: Ladies Hairdresser' offering cheap perms to pensioners on Thursdays.

A few years ago, I interviewed fifty of the tower-block residents. Most of them had been uprooted from slum areas in the city centre, from the rows of terraces and back-to-backs where social life happens on the street and in the corner shop. In Millbrook they had cramped lifts (out of order as often as not) and concrete staircases instead of the street, and they were poor substitutes. Most of the people I spoke to complained of theft and vandalism: you could never leave your shopping with the pram, never hang clothes in the communal drying areas. A surprising number did not know any of their neighbours. The thin walls, and the 'scissors design' which makes every bedroom back on to a corridor, meant that people's most frequent contact with their neighbours was having their sleep disturbed by next door's brawling children. The petty larceny of stolen milk, and, worse, milk-money, bred an incipient paranoia about the malevolent habits of the people across the corridor.

Here social worlds were shrinking: often the most common contact with someone outside the flat was the weekly visit to or from a mother or father in the city centre. Church groups in Millbrook hardly begin to dent the neurotic privacy behind which so many of the place's inhabitants have taken to biding. The stay-at-home mother in a tower-block flat can be as alone as an astronaut marooned in space: indeed, the sociological space in which she moves is almost as uncharted.

The densely interwoven street-life of the traditional city (or the life of the Italian piazza, really the living-room of the apartments around the square) has always been feared by the middle classes: who knows what unpleasant radical ideas might not be brewed up in those hugger-mugger enclaves of the proletariat? Tower-block planning, by driving people into disconnected private cells, reliably insures against mass insurrections. Bad neighbours make for a certain kind of social security; Millbrook breeds vandals, but not revolutionaries.

The Sun City and Radiant City – really the same place – are both expressions of apprehension, disgust, and despair, and we should not fall for the assumption that utopias are usually the work of optimists. Far more often they are thinly veiled cries of rage and disappointment. Millbrook is, of course, something less – an expression of funk, piety; and the exercise of a deficient imagination. Were one to read the place as a novel, one might say that the author had read and copied all the fashionable books without understanding them, and had produced a typical minor work in which all the passions and prejudices of the current masterpieces were unconsciously and artlessly reflected. It is full of heartless innocence, a terrible place to live precisely because none of its effects are truly willed.

But it does piously reflect the moral extremes, the melodrama, which has so afflicted modern town-planning. A city is a very bad place which one might convert into a very good place, a dangerous place to be made safe, a black place to be coloured green. The answer to the terraced, two-up, two-down house is a grey skyscraper with its head lost in the clouds; to the crowded street, a stretch of unbroken grass big enough to fight a war on; to the corner grocer's, a yawning shopping plaza. Behind all these strategies lie a savage contempt for the city and an arrogant desire to refashion human society into almost any shape other than the one we have at present.

The planners have grasped a single truth. They have recognised that in the city they are dealing with some hugely enlarged frame for human behaviour in which moral extremes are likely to be the norm. The city, they sense, is the province of rogues and angels, and a style of building, or a traffic scheme, might tip it conclusively in one or the other direction. More to the point, it is a place where individuals are so little known that they can be conveniently transmuted into moral ciphers. A man who designs a farm has to know a little about the farmer – whether he has cows, or pigs, or grain. He has to know the pattern of his day, his movements from one building to another. He has to understand the living requirements of different species of animals. But a man who designs a city can make up his people as arbitrarily as a novelist in identical batches of thousands at a time. And if he works in the service of the state or the local authority, he tends to create his characters in the images of insensible oafs, inspired by indifference, softened by chronic inactivity. His architecture is supposed to anaesthetise or ameliorate these glibly imagined moral characteristics. If people stick cautiously to the edges of the shopping plaza and never use the paved space provided at the centre, or if they prefer a bus ride and a real city supermarket to the overpriced minimarket he has allocated them, then they are at fault – they have not learned to live in a city that ought, for them, to be ideal.

If architects tend to see us as opaque wisps or rude diagrams, they are, perhaps, doing no more than falling into a characteristically urban habit of mind, a way of thinking and feeling about other people which the conditions of the city make particularly easy. Finding the city a bad place, and suspiciously viewing its citizens as potential wastrels and villains, are responses which proceed out of a basic and widespread nervousness about the kind of moral drama which the city forces us to participate in.

For in a community of strangers, we need a quick, easy-to-use set of stereotypes, cartoon outlines, with which to classify the people we encounter. In a village, most of the people you deal with have been known to you (or to someone in your family circle) for a long time; they have matured subtly and slowly as characters, and are painted in varying shades of grey. You will probably have seen them in more than one role: the milkman or the postman is not just the man who delivers milk or mail, he is known too for a variety of off-duty interests and occupations. He is, you happen to know, a keen gardener, his marriage is reputed to be rocky; he is just out of hospital after an operation. My city milkman, though, happens fully fledged: a uniform hat, a smudge of moustache, a rounding belly … I have no more to go on. Most of the time I need no more: the city is a great deadener of curiosity. But, if, for instance, I am thinking of buying something from one of these patchy strangers, I have to guess at his history, try instantly to gauge his moral and emotional qualities. All I have to help me is my subjective knowledge of accents, clothes, brands of car, my reactions to endomorphic or ectomorphic figures: external signs and signals from which I construct the character with whom I am going to deal. Is he good or bad? A truth-teller or a liar? Lecherous or chaste? An actor, a bookie, a clerk, a dimwit, an enemy …?

People who live in cities become expert at making these rapid, subconscious decisions. At any large party, one can see people 'reading' strangers with the abstracted speed of a blind man tracing over a book in Braille. Mechanical aids to such character-reading are at a premium in cities. The rise of the industrial city in the nineteenth century coincided with the craze for phrenology and palmistry. At any bookstall today one can find several cheap pamphlets on graphology and quasi-scientific disquisitions on the relationship between body-shape and moral character. There is a vast market for cranky guides to person-spotting, guides that correspond, worryingly closely, to those charts designed for idle children showing the silhouettes of every aeroplane in the world. Judgments have to be made fast, and almost any judgment will do. The riot of amateur astrology we have suffered from recently is one of the more annoying expressions of this city hunger for quick ways of classifying people.

'What are you?' says the girl in the caftan, then, impatiently, 'No, I mean what's your *sign*?'

Gemini, Taurus, Aries, Libra … a character synopsis for everyone. Margot has initiative and tact, a strong sense of loyalty and a need to conform; Derek is creative, ambitious, and self-confident, seeks harmony in personal relationships, but needs help in money matters.

The great urban visual art is the cartoon. In Gillray, Hogarth, Rowlandson and Cruikshank, the people of the city are portrayed with exactly that physical and moral exaggeration with which girls who are 'into' astrology endow the men they meet at parties. They are very thin or very fat, giants or dwarfs, excessively angelic or excessively corrupted. Emblems tell everything: Hogarth's idle apprentice, for example, is known by his clay pipe, his open collar, the jug of ale on his loom, and the page from Moll Flanders pinned up over his head. These public signs compose all that we need to know of his character.

In Dickens, our greatest urban novelist, the physical shape of someone is a continuing part of his personality. People appear in his novels as they might appear on a street or in a party, equipped with a set of dimensions and a name which we learn later. In *Our Mutual Friend,* Bradley Headstone is huge, coarse and slablike; Jenny Wren is a tiny cripple; Rumty Wilfer is pink and roly-poly. And, however much the characters change and emerge during the course of the novel, we are constantly reminded of these initial cartoon images. They carry their personal stereotypes with them like grotesque, gaily-painted husks – even when, morally, they have outgrown them. How different this is from a novelist like Jane Austen, in whose work the closer you get to a character, the less visible is his external, easy-to-spot carapace. Most writers use caricature for their background characters: Dickens foregrounds the technique, and makes caricature something which the characters themselves have to lug, often unhappily, through the plot. R. Wilfer wishes he wasn't so infuriatingly round, pink, and ineffectual; Bradley Headstone rages against being so damningly associated with graveyards and dark, thickset emotions. Yet that is how people in cities are recognised again and again by every new acquaintance, by every observer of the crowd; and Dickens's characters simply have to put up with their dwarfishness, their wooden legs, and their toppling craggy heights. To be merely grey, especially subtly grey, in a city, is not to be seen at all.

Both cities themselves and the people who live in them are subject to this convenient distortion and exaggeration. Both fall easy prey to that impulse, which besets almost everyone who writes about urban life, to find a fixing synecdoche, to substitute a simple lurid part for a bafflingly complex whole. In a world of crowds and strangers, where things happen at speed, are glimpsed and cannot be recalled – a world, in short, which is simply too big to be held at one time in one's imagination – synecdoche is much more than a rhetorical figure, it is a means of survival.

To call a city a slough of despond, or a great wen, or a cesspool, is to give it a functional identity, to fix it in the mind as surely as Bradley Headstone is fixed in Dickens's novel. The city, like the people in it, lends itself to this sort of moral abstraction. Oddly enough, cities, for all their bigness and complexity, get tagged with hard-edged images much more readily than small towns. What mental picture is conjured by, say, Chicago or Sheffield? Isn't it more definite, more dominant, than that of Banbury? A line of cattle trucks, a lamplit street, a waterfront of cranes, are emblematic substitutes for the contrary lines of millions of individual lives. Moral fervour – seeing a particular city as especially evil, a sink of quite unprecedented iniquity – may be a simple convenience, a way of glueing together those visual fragments that compose the city in our head. The sheer imaginative cumbersomeness of the city makes us frequently incapable of distinguishing its parts from its whole; and moral synecdoche, the utopia/dystopia syndrome, is part of our essential habit of mind when we think about it. One might add that, in England, the single feature of the city which has adhered most strongly to writers' minds is its dirt, and dirt is one of the few objects whose moral connotation is as definite and public as its physical characteristics. The presence of dirt provides us with the elusive key we have been seeking, and the English have been quick to seize on dirt as the single defining quality of the big city. Charles Kingsley, who was no slouch on inner cleanliness, wrote in 1857:

> The social state of a city depends directly on its moral state, and – I
> fear dissenting voices, but I must say what I believe to be truth – that
> the moral state of a city depends – how far I know not, but frightfully,
> to an extent uncalculated, and perhaps uncalculable – in the physical
> state of that city; on the food, water, air, and lodging of its inhabitants.

Kingsley wrote a series of bad novels in which he explored the filth and disease of London and, by way of contrast, sketchily adumbrated the alternative kingdom of sweetness and light. The original metaphor was Augustine's, but Kingsley worked at it with fanatical literal-mindedness. Fogs, smogs, stinks, suppurations, chimneys (swept by consumptively angelic little boys), stains, lumps of raw sewage … this was London, and very convenient it was too. Seeing the city in its turds was the simple synecdoche of a simple moralist, and Kingsley throve on it hysterically. (The most vivid, and clearly most enjoyably written, chapter of *Alton Locke* concerns a delirious victim of cholera sitting by the side of a reeking open sewer and talking of the rats which have grossly disfigured the bodies of his wife and children.)

People with more elaborate minds have been more inventive with the form. Dickens loves and exploits synecdoche, and identifies it especially with the new energetic middle class who were making over the industrial city for their own ends. They were – and are – the people quickest to label others simply by their functions, who saw that the city offered a ready-made theatre for fast, opportunistic self-aggrandisement. These people could capitalise on the speed and superficiality of London's social and business life; people who acted on appearances, who, to all intents and purposes, *were* appearances. Dickens called these 'bran-new' people the Veneerings, nicely linking them with that other Victorian craze for marquetry.

> Mr and Mrs Veneering were bran-new people in a bran-new house in a bran-new quarter of London. Everything about the Veneerings was spick and span new. All their furniture was new, all their friends were new, all their servants were new, their plate was new, their carriage was new, their harness was new, they themselves were new, they were as newly married as was lawfully compatible with their having a bran-new baby, and if they had set up a great-grandfather, he would have come home in matting from the Pantechnicon, without a scratch on him, French polished to the crown of his head.

When the Veneerings give a dinner party, they do not invite people: rather, they acquire, 'an innocent piece of dinner furniture' called Twemlow, 'a Member, an Engineer, a Payer-off of the National Debt, a Poem on Shakespeare, a Grievance, and a Public Office'. How simplified does society thus become, its members concisely labelled by the single role you want them to play and which, hopefully, you may exploit. Here Dickens is satirising a whole way of seeing and acting in the city: we pick someone out from the crowd because they possess one significant functional quality. This feature turns into all the person is: it turns him into a living Rowlandson grotesque – a walking nose, a pair of sated bulbous lips let out on their own, while their parent mind and body stay home minding the dog.

It is no coincidence that synecdoche provides the basis of the moral melodrama – the play in which Envy, Sloth, Anger, Lust, Pride, Virtue, and Heroism compete for the soul of Everyman. Once we treat people, morally and functionally, in terms of single synecdochal roles, we turn both our lives and theirs into a formal drama. The city itself becomes an allegorical backdrop, painted with symbols of the very good and the very evil. The characters who strut before it similarly take on exaggerated colourings. Isolated from their personal histories, glaringly illuminated by the concentrated light of a single defining concern, under constant interrogation from their fellows, these urban people turn, unwittingly, into actors. They saw the air, their faces are thick in greasepaint, they live the disembodied stage-life of pierrots – who knows or cares where they sleep or eat? Their reality lies solely in their performance. When Saint Augustine castigated the Romans for going to the theatre, he accused them of 'playing a madder part now than ever before', as if a double theatre was involved – as if the audience at the circus was itself enacting a riotous drama. The dutch-picture recedes into infinitude: actors applaud actors applauding actors …

It is surely in recognition of this intrinsic theatricality of city life that public places in the city so often resemble stages awaiting a scenario. At dinner time in London, people strip off their working clothes and uniforms, and put on the costumes that go with being a character. Out come bangles, neckerchiefs, broad-brimmed hats, wild coloured jackets with jackboots to match. In any restaurant, one can find people taking to self-expression with histrionic fervour, giving themselves over to monologues and dramatic scenes which, to judge by their volume, seem to be intended not for their immediate companions at all, but for the city at large – that uncountable audience of strangers.

I have in mind an expensive mock-up of an Italian *trattoria* in South Kensington: low-slung lighting, strings of empty Chianti bottles, bread-sticks in tumblers, and conically folded napkins of unearthly whiteness and rigidity. Although the tables are arranged in a maze of low, white-wood cubicles with potted ferns growing out of ice buckets, this is not at all a private place. The fanciful cubicles rather enhance the atmosphere of a public spectacle, like chalk marks on a stage showing where separate blocks or groups of actors ought to stand. Everyone is visible and within earshot of everybody else. To enter, one has to be checked in by a florid waiter at the desk, one's way barred by a sumptuously scrolled hatstand. Thus newcomers are subjected to a ritual which calls everyone's attention to the arrival of these new characters in the drama; and the cross-talk of the waiters – delivered in a style of gamey operatic *recitatif* – makes the waiting group an embarrassed centre of disturbance.

At one table, I am sitting with a girl; in the cubicle across the narrow aisle, a middle-aged couple are with a younger woman; they're in their trim early fifties, scented, polished and silver grey, she is in her thirties, tangled, nervous, chain-smoking. At my side glance, her voice pauses, then intensifies in volume and expression. 'My thing was self-absorption. Eric couldn't take it.' The couple with her look across at us, a little abashed. But the woman is set for her aria, and the addition of an audience of strangers turns the story of her divorce into a vibrant, plotted skein, a work of dramatic self-exposure.

'… a twenty-two-year-old acid freak who'd gone through a whole shipful of sailors between Algiers and Southampton!'

The man comes in, lugubriously jovial, crying his voice out for pitch: 'Ghastly. Oh, ghastly. But what exactly did you do about the bottle of rose hip syrup?'

'… I wouldn't have minded so awfully if he hadn't sneaked off in the Cortina. I'd got everything at Sainsbury's that morning and the bastard didn't even take the shopping out of the boot.'

My friend picks sourly at her cocktail. The middle-aged woman across the way finds something to hunt for in her handbag. But the man, the divorcée and I are set for a three-act meal. Everybody's voice rises. I start telling a boring restaurant story to my companion, but I can feel it growing loud and contrived, intended for public consumption. My friend responds with an exaggeratedly intimate whisper so that I have to bend to her face to listen. The younger woman does a proficient travesty of her husband's hippie mistress, loose-mouthed, blurry-eyed. The man, a little uneasy now at the extravagance of his friend's display, turns to his wife and tries to involve her in the conversation, but she won't be drawn. At a particularly juicy moment in the divorce story, his eyes click up to my friend, who registers him with a tight smile. At another juncture the woman is apparently delivering her monologue for me alone, and I grin cautiously.

This particular dinner ended with a suitably outrageous symbol. The waiter had brought round a plate of those Italian bonbons wrapped in patterned rice-paper. The divorcée wanted to watch her paper burn. She smoothed it out, folded it into a squat cylinder, and stood it on end in a saucer. The waiter lit it. It was a piece of pure ritual: the paper flared green and blue, then flounced into the air, hovering for a moment between the two tables in the dark space above the hanging lamps. The divorcée laughed, the man laughed, his wife pulled a polite grimace, I laughed, my friend smiled in complicity with the wife. The waiter (an expert stage manager, tipped heavily for his collusion in the show) stood tolerantly by. It was a burst of rigged applause at the end of a performance.

Such improvised, crass theatre could only have happened among strangers. Like real theatre, it broke with social conventions, allowed the participants to communicate things to each other which are not licit in normal circumstances. But a city, judged in terms of our social behaviour inside it, is not a normal circumstance; and its public arenas – restaurants, late night trains, certain streets and squares, like Piccadilly Circus in London – are licensed for a degree of theatrical abnormality.

In cities, people are given to acting, putting on a show of themselves. And it was in recognition of this fact that Plato saw imitation as a major vice to be stamped out from the city. He was convinced that drama, spontaneous or rehearsed, corrupts the actor. The role you play, he argued, too easily turns into all you are. In Book Three of *The Republic,* Socrates says: 'Did you never observe how imitations, beginning in early youth and continuing far into life, at length grow into habits and become a second nature, affecting body, voice, and mind?' He goes on to describe the lowest sort of actor, the man who will accept any part he is offered:

> Nothing will be too bad for him: and he will be ready to imitate anything, in right good earnest and before a large company. As I was just now saying, he will attempt to represent the roll of thunder, the noise of wind and hail, or the creaking of wheels and pulleys, and the various sounds of flutes, pipes, trumpets, and all sorts of instruments: he will bark like a dog, bleat like a sheep, or crow like a cock; his entire art will consist of imitation of voice and gesture, or will be but slightly blended with narration.

The condition of chronic impersonation portrayed by Plato has always afflicted the city. As we try to grasp it as an imaginative whole, we endow it with exaggerated, Manichean qualities of unique goodness and unique evil. Our own characters distort; we grow in size, but the growth is of a single feature. At any one time, we are likely to perform like the gross types of a comedy of humours: Lechery now, tomorrow Wit, or Sentiment, or Melancholy. The newcomer to the city has to learn to live on a perpetually inflated scale, to adapt himself to these highly coloured projections of spontaneous melodrama.

Mirko Zardini

Toward a Sensorial Urbanism

In recent years, numerous studies have taken up the theme of the city and the urban domain. It seems that the city can no longer be avoided: as the predominant setting of our daily lives, it is "everywhere and in everything."[1] The notion of urbanism as a way of life, independent of the physical density of the environment and thus not dependent on locale, is becoming a concrete reality.[2]

During the 1960s and 1970s, studies and descriptions of the city focused mainly on changes of scale, on the surprising growth that led to the emergence of novel urban configurations. New terms such as metropolitan region, city-region, megalopolis, or megistopolis[3] gradually began to replace traditional references like city, town, *ville, cité, città, Stadt, urbs,* and *polis,* and even metropolis or *Grosstadt,* which were no longer considered adequate to describe the new conurbations. Studies and descriptions of the last decades have attempted to represent the new qualities and increased complexity of urban phenomena. To suggest these new conditions, authors have resorted to adjectives or nouns modifying the word "city."[4] It is clear from the diverse viewpoints these represent that a unified vision of the urban has been renounced in the face of the complexity of the phenomena being observed and analyzed.

So numerous are the studies and the terms coined in service of this new effort of description and interpretation that they would fill not one but several dictionaries on the subject of the contemporary city. In effect, they betray a Borgesian urge to capture the nature of the contemporary urban context in terms that run the alphabetical gamut from A to Z: anxious city; city of bits; compact or cyber city; dual or dead city or *città disfatta;* edge, edgier, or entrepreneurial, or event city; fantasy city; generic, global, or green city; hypercity; instant city; Japanese city; kitsch city; *cité locale* or lettered city; Manga or mortal city; *ville narcisse* or network city; open city or ökotop Stadt; *ville panique,* partitioned city, or *città pulpa;* city of quartz; rat *ville*; survival city; soft or sun city; tourist, television, or thematic city; unknown city; virtual city; wounded city; x or Xerox city; year city; *Zwischenstadt* or *zweckentfremdet.*[5] Despite their diversity of approach, all of these studies reveal how the cities in which we live have changed, how our ways of looking at the city have changed, and above all, how we ourselves have changed.

Contemporary City Planning and Environment

Urbanistic studies and urban projects have also attempted to define new strategies of intervention that are capable of effecting transformations of the urban fabric, and of responding to new problems posed by the forces of globalization, de-localization, and fragmentation. From new urbanism to post-urbanism or re-urbanism, from everyday urbanism to informal urbanism, and from eco-urbanism to landscape urbanism, a range of new definitions have been assigned to contemporary city planning in recent years.[6] The multiplicity of these designations clearly reflects the wide range of responses and approaches adopted in the face of new urban phenomena worldwide.

New urbanism, for example, has responded to the rediscovery of social and environmental needs with the often nostalgic revival of certain models of the historic city. Post-urbanism, in the Eisenmanian sense of the term, emphasizes above all the value of the project as a means of critiquing the *status quo* without distinguishing between architecture and city planning. This overlap between the two, tied to a vision of the city that is not just morphological, but also social and political, is also manifest in Manuel de Solà-Morales's research on the urban project, the urban section, and the theme of urban corners. For De Solà-Morales's, in fact, the corner is at once a building, an urban place, and a metaphor for the city, as a place of meeting and confrontation between "diverse people."[7] This is a theme that recurs in many lines of inquiry. In particular, it resonates in projects belonging to what has been called everyday urbanism,[8] inspired by the rediscovery of quotidian life in the work of Henri Lefebvre, Michel de Certeau, and Guy Debord, in which the daily reality of the city's inhabitants becomes the centre of interest. Even though the themes of advocacy or grassroots participation in architecture and city planning that were so prominent in the 1960s and 1970s are not explicitly referenced, it is clear that attention is focused largely on the informal city, and that the goal is a democratic approach to planning, from the bottom up.

There is now widespread interest in the environmental and ecological issues confronting cities, in particular sustainability and biodiversity, and a renewed and general faith in the efficacy of the tools and methods of landscape design to bring about the understanding and transformation of the urban environment. It is not just a question of a reappropriation of the technical instruments, something that is not new, if we look at the experiences of the 19th and early 20th centuries, but rather a conceptual change: we have moved from Boccioni's "city that rises" to the "landscape that advances," metaphorically as well as actually.[9] As a result, Iñaki Ábalos and Juan Herreros can claim that "every location has begun to be regarded as a landscape, either natural or artificial."[10]

This great variety of studies, strategies, and projects notwithstanding, are we not missing something? If we look back to the late 1960s and 1970s, we find that the theme of the urban environment was already at the centre of many prescient reflections, most considered radical at the time. However disparate were the viewpoints of that era, from the technological optimism of Buckminster Fuller to the social criticism of collectives like Superstudio, the urban environment seems to have been examined in a broader and more complex manner than in recent decades.[11] Investigations into phenomenology, for example, though they may not have had widespread impact in the field at large, have surely been a crucial point of departure for theorists like Juhani Pallasmaa and others. This strongly suggests the need for a rethinking of proposals dating from these years, especially because they were framed by political and social issues, debates, and events whose gravity is mirrored by events that are overwhelming cities today. Cedric Price, Charles Moore, Christian Norberg-Schulz, Kevin Lynch, Superstudio, Gordon Matta-Clark, and Alison and Peter Smithson, for example, all raised questions and engaged themes that are resurfacing today. What is clear is that some of the most innovative proposals of the 1970s exceeded our capacity to realize them at the time, whereas today, they seem not only relevant, but also feasible as events on a global scale transform both the landscape of cities and the hierarchy of our priorities on a daily basis.

For example, studies and proposals of the 1970s which dealt with the qualities of atmosphere, nature and the environment, the human body and health – including those of Cedric Price, who observed that "mental, physical, and sensory well-being is required"[12] – are once again at the centre of debates concerning the city, because the improvement of the quality of the urban environment is now more than ever a necessity. It is not a matter of returning to a conception of the environment as purely climatic fact or visual phenomenon, as with the British townscape of the 1960s and 1970s,[13] but rather of proposing a broader view of the environment that takes into consideration the full spectrum of perceptual phenomena that make up the sensorial dimension *beyond the regime of the visual.* Material and tactile properties, the control of temperature, humidity, and odours, along with acoustic qualities, are increasingly considered fundamental to the definition of private spaces. Unfortunately, this is not yet the case with urban spaces.

Public Space and "Sensorial" Streets

The shrinking and impoverishment of so-called public space is now a prominent theme in contemporary debates. Some of the activities once carried out in public space have been taken over by new forms of communal space (i.e., space that is privately owned but in public use, such as shopping malls or theme parks),[14] while other functions of communication and entertainment that originated as communal have been transferred to the private sphere by means of the television and computer. Today, one predominant concern seems to be determining the character of contemporary urban space: *security.* The open spaces of the city, streets and squares, along with communal spaces, have above all become spaces of fear, and thus, inevitably, spaces of control. Fear is a primary force driving the proliferation of socially homogeneous and controlled enclaves, gated communities, and theme parks. And it is fear that determines the definition of what is left of public space.

To keep fear – all the various forms of fear that have possessed us – at bay, we have resorted to remedies such as the illumination of public space, its enclosure and segregation, and video surveillance. According to Steven Flusty, certain characteristics are introduced into urban spaces in order to make them repellent to the public. Flusty's discouraging list includes: "stealthy spaces" (spaces that cannot be found); "slippery spaces" (spaces that cannot be reached); "crusty spaces" (spaces that cannot be accessed); "prickly spaces" (spaces that cannot be comfortably occupied); and "jittery spaces" (spaces that cannot be utilized unobserved).[15] Contemporary architecture and city planning are increasingly preoccupied with masking such responses and repressing the conceptual as well as real nature of new systems of control. Zygmunt Baumann points out that, on the contrary, urban space ought to be shaped by the concept of "mixophilia," to favour and encourage the possibility "of living peacefully and happily with difference, and taking advantage of the variety of stimuli."[16] To achieve this end, it would be necessary to promote "the diffusion of public spaces that are open, inviting, and hospitable, spaces that citizens of all kinds would be tempted to make frequent use of and to share intentionally and willingly."[17] What qualities should these spaces have? Is it possible to transform the urban spaces described by Flusty into liveable, appealing, and interesting environments?

As early as the 1960s, in her critique of planning practices, Jane Jacobs suggested some possible qualities of the urban environment, stressing the importance of difference, of the human dimension, and insisting on the role of the street as public space.[18] In his influential text of the 1980s, William H. Whyte also proposed the street and the square as public spaces *par excellence,* analyzing their modes of use and their various components, from water to wind, from trees to light, from shade to sun, arriving at the idea of a "sensorial street."[19]

Nonetheless, city planning has long privileged qualities of urban space based exclusively on visual perception. Whether the aim was to define a regular space through control of alignments and heights or through definition of materials and colours, or to accentuate contrasts and differences in a picturesque vision of the urban environment, the eye has always been privileged. The same consideration has not been given to the ear and nose (nor the sense of touch). Above all, sounds and odours have been considered disturbing elements, and architecture and city planning have exclusively been concerned with marginalizing them, covering them up, or eliminating them altogether.

From the Hygienic City to Smellscapes and Soundscapes

This process of sanitization of the urban environment, although it was prefigured at the dawn of the Italian Renaissance by Leonardo Bruni in his "Panegyric to the City of Florence" (*circa* 1403–4),[20] is only taken up in earnest at the level of the municipality in the mid-eighteenth century.[21] The transformation of the character and quality of public space starts with the first regulations concerning street cleaning and attempts to control the proliferation of dust and mud by paving streets with stone, and subsequently, asphalt. Even with respect to garbage collection and the elimination of dirt and odours, the visual aspect of the intervention, whether it was paving or plastering, assumed a predominant role, often in excess of what was actually required.[22]

This dual preoccupation with the visual and the "hygienic" has been a constant factor in the shaping of attitudes toward the modern city, and it persists today. Thus, the paving of roads and squares, street lighting, and regulations to prevent the spread of unpleasant odours and noises were just the first step in the ongoing process of embellishing public space.[23] With the introduction and dissemination of new technologies (now on an increasingly global scale), and the consequent production of new and more or less undesirable effects of a sensory nature, solutions considered optimal at one moment come to be perceived as problematic, in and of themselves, at a later point. This is the case with asphalt, which is now blamed for the increase in automobile traffic, and also street lighting, which has resulted in excessive illumination of the city at night.

Nonetheless, the continuous erosion of the perceptual sphere, by sanitization on the one hand and standardization on the other, has to contend with olfactory and aural distinctions, which however impalpable, have turned out to be highly resistant. The processes of globalization and the diffusion of now-common odours (that mixture of gasoline, detergents, plumbing, and junk food of which Ivan Illich speaks)[24] notwithstanding, every city and every place still has its own smellscape: "There is a smell of London. There is a Russian smell … There is a smell of Central Europe … There are scents of the Mediterranean and the Orient … There is the subtlety of the odours of India … There are the odours of China … There is the smell of America," observes André Siegfried, one of the first writers to take an interest in the geography of colours, odours, and sounds.[25] Likewise, the research of R. Murray Schafer and Laboratoire Cresson has focused on the study of diversity in soundscapes of urban environments.[26] Thus, alongside the traditional notion of a visual landscape, we have begun to recognize the identity of individual cities by their unique sounds and smells. One need only look at the recent rise in recorded soundscapes as a form of "guide" to cities around the world, or the insightful sound installations and "walks" of Canadian artist Janet Cardiff, to grasp the importance of this new alertness to sounds and noises in the urban environment.

Architecture and Sensorial Experience

It is not just the urban setting in which we live that changes with the passing of time: our own perceptions, sensitivities, and ways of life, as well as our sensory thresholds and levels of tolerance or appreciation of odours, sounds, dirt, darkness, cold, or heat tend to vary. However, this variation in perception and sensitivity, and thus judgement, does not depend solely on time, but also on location and culture.[27] The abstract idea of a modern human being who prefers, for example, to live at an ambient temperature of 18 °C has resulted in a multitude of contemporary human beings who live in different places and cultures, with different levels of awareness and tolerance.[28] In contrast to what Charles Moore suggested in the 1970s,[29] we do not "live" in a generic body, but in bodies that differ widely in their perceptual culture and capacities, and that are sometimes even modified by technological prostheses. As David Howes has observed in connection with Marshall McLuhan's research, "perception is not just a matter of biology, psychology, or personal history, but of cultural formation."[30] In recent years, the human and social sciences, from anthropology to geography, have undergone a "sensorial revolution" in which the "senses" constitute not so much a new field of study as a fundamental shift in the mode and media we employ to observe and define our own fields of study.

Much of contemporary architecture shares this renewed interest in a sensorial experience extending beyond the purely visual realm. Architects including Gaetano Pesce, Jacques Herzog, Juhani Pallasmaa, Steven Holl, Kengo Kuma, and even Peter Eisenman have pointed out that too much importance is given to the visual aspect of architecture. "Yes, sound, material, not just vision. What I'm trying to do is to question the dominance of vision and this is a difficult thing because most people are judged by the visual image. There is too much visual noise in our environment for me," remarked Peter Eisenman in a recent interview.[31]

In their description of the "conglomerate order," Alison and Peter Smithson hypothesized that a building can "harnesses all the senses: it can accept a certain roughness, it can operate at night; it can offer, especially, pleasures beyond the eyes: they are perhaps the pleasures of territory that the other animals feel so strongly."[32]

Contemporary interiors – from hospitals to the communal spaces of shopping malls, theme parks, and places of entertainment and consumption – devote particular attention to differences in sensory perception, and many are conceived specifically as extensions of marketing strategies for consumer goods and experiences. A growing number of the objects that surround us are designed with a special emphasis on their sensual characteristics. In the field of communication of abstract information, for example, Saul Wurman's information design[33] has been superseded by new research that focuses on multi-sensory design, introducing the aspects of sound and touch as well.[34] This interest is currently even influencing the design of virtual environments. For example, the Sensory Environments Evaluation (SEE)

Project, renouncing the photorealism of the past twenty years, "seeks to formulate a new design methodology for virtual environments that utilize multiple sensory inputs to induce presence."[35] In a highly successful book entitled *The Experience Economy*,[36] Joseph Pine, II, and James Gilmore suggest, as a first step toward rendering merchandise more experiential, and therefore more interesting and valuable, intensifying the customer's sensorial interaction with the goods themselves.[37]

At a moment when sensory marketing, purveyors of the experience economy, and the practice of multi-sensory design, not to mention the crucial investigations of contemporary artists, seem to be devoting so much attention to sensorial experience, it is paradoxical to find that the urban environment remains untouched by this sort of consideration.

Character, Atmosphere, and Sensorial Urbanism

Critical thinking in this context is no longer driven by language, semiotics, text, and signs, but by a rediscovery of phenomenology, experience, the body, perceptions, and the senses. This "sensorial revolution" has been matched in architecture and urbanism by a rediscovery of the element of character.[38] Associated with a particular place, the term *character* indicates its specificity; at the same time it does not refer to an exclusively visual condition, but embraces all the various sensory experiences that one can have in a place. As far back as the 1970s, Kevin Lynch[39] and Christian Norberg-Schulz reintroduced this theme into their reflections on the urban environment. In particular, Norberg-Schulz described place as a "total" qualitative phenomenon, making use of expressions like "environmental character" and "atmosphere."[40]

It is precisely this last term that is increasingly being used to describe the environmental qualities of a place.[41] Gernot Böhme has portrayed *atmosphere* as an almost objective condition. It implies the physical presence of the subject and the object; it focuses attention on place; and above all, it presupposes a sensory experience. Böhme has observed that "sensory perception as opposed to judgment is rehabilitated in aesthetics, and the term 'aesthetic' is restored to its original meaning, namely the theory of perception."[42] Yet it is not just a question of developing a new sensitivity. As Reinhard Knodt has pointed out, specific expertise is also necessary, an expertise that is extended to the practical field through the work of artists, architects, city planners, or landscape designers.[43] In establishing a "sensorial city planning" that is capable of defining the character and atmosphere of places, it is necessary to avoid a practice based, once again, on vision. The discipline of landscape design cannot help in this regard, for it, too, like architecture and city planning, is dominated by the eye. Unfortunately, as Iñaki Ábalos points out, "true picturesque invention – in which places have a voice and speak to us, telling us what they expect to become, what they need or do not need – has developed … as pure appearances, as cosmetics."[44]

According to Kengo Kuma, there is another, non-visual practice to which we can turn for reference in this regard: "The practice of gardening provides us with many hints and gives us the courage."[45] In fact, it is not just a matter of reducing our dependence on vision and introducing richer conditions of perception; there is also the need to "make manifest that totality called *place*."[46] The gardener is always in the garden, he is practically its prisoner. There being no distance between him and the garden, he cannot manipulate it visually from the outside, as a landscape designer would do. "He is forever occupied with watering, ridding plants of bugs, weeding and replanting, and the garden would cease to exist if he stopped … There is no temporal *point* where a goal is reached and completion is achieved. There is no completion for a garden."[47]

The materials, projects, and studies presented in *Sense of the City* (2005) at the Canadian Centre for Architecture propose a different way of talking about, describing, and planning our cities;[48] they suggest thinking of them as places for our bodies (and our souls);[49] they remind us how mutable is our way of perceiving the urban environment; they offer us a history of the changes in the Western city from new points of view that have been hitherto neglected; in addition, they reveal to us the possibilities provided by the urban environment in its various aspects – those of sound, smell, touch, vision, and climate – and invite us to look at them in new ways.

The physical urban environment, despite the impoverishment to which it is currently subject, is in fact a vital part of our human experience. As Joseph Rykwert points out, the seduction of place still exists, and the spread of cyberspace will not be able to substitute for "the functions of the tangible public realm."[50] On the contrary, it is precisely the expansion of the virtual, globally connected world that renders specific places increasingly appealing and thus important. The fact that accessibility is no longer the discriminating factor makes the other qualities of a place fundamental to its ability to attract.[51]

Thus atmosphere, character, and sensorial qualities are becoming key factors in the definition of a place, even from an economic perspective. All the more reason for us to demand that this attention be turned to public places, and to urban spaces in general. Is it possible to combine the different approaches to contemporary urbanism with a "sensorial urbanism," capable of offering a broader understanding of urban settings, interested in describing the character and atmosphere of places, and aiming to contribute to a new definition of public space? Alongside conceptions of the city as a place of difference, conflict, and confrontation, is it not possible to develop an approach to the city as a place of camaraderie, conviviality, and comfort?

Notes

1   See the introduction to Ash Amin and Nigel Thrift. *Cities: Reimagining the Urban.* Cambridge: Polity Press, 2002.

2   See Louis Wirth. "Urbanism as a Way of Life." In *The American Journal of Sociology,* Vol. 44, No. 1, 1938, and Melvin M. Webber. "The Urban Place and the Nonplace Urban Realm." In *Explorations into Urban Structure,* edited by Melvin M. Webber et al., Philadelphia: University of Pennsylvania Press, 1964.

3   Gottmann, Jean. *Megalopolis: The Urbanized Northeastern Seaboard of the United States.* New York: Twentieth Century Fund, 1961. The term "megistopolis" was coined by Gottmann in a 1978 essay entitled "How Large Can Cities Grow?" reprinted in *Since Megalopolis: The Urban Writings of Jean Gottmann,* edited by Jean Gottmann and Robert A. Harper. Baltimore & London: Johns Hopkins University Press, 1990.

4   In this connection, see Nan Ellin. "Slash City." In *Lotus international* 110, September 2001: 58–72.

5   For a hypothetical dictionary on the contemporary city, see Ludovica Molo and Mirko Zardini, eds. "La città contemporanea dalla A alla Z." In *archi* February 1999: 10–45. The compilation of dictionaries is an increasingly common practice today. For a different interpretation, see *The Metapolis Dictionary of Advanced Architecture.* Barcelona: Actar, 2003.

6   A series of seminars held at the University of Michigan in 2004 offered a first and very interesting panorama; see Rahul Mehrotra, ed. *Everyday Urbanism: Margaret Crawford vs. Michael Speaks.* Ann Arbor: University of Michigan Press & A. Alfred Taubman College of Architecture, 2005, and Robert Fishman, ed. *New Urbanism: Peter Calthorpe vs. Lars Lerup.* Ann Arbor: University of Michigan Press, 2005, and Roy Strickland, ed. *Post Urbanism and Reurbanism: Peter Eisenman vs. Barbara Littenberg and Steven Peterson – Designs for Ground Zero.* Ann Arbor: University of Michigan Press, 2005. For the debate on landscape, see James Corner, ed. *Recovering Landscape: Essays in Contemporary Landscape Architecture.* New York: Princeton Architectural Press, 1999, and Mohsen Mostafavi and Ciro Najle, eds. *Landscape Urbanism: A Manual for the Machinic Landscape.* London: AA Publications, 2003.

7   De Solà-Morales, Manuel. *Ciudades, esquinas = Cities, Corners,* exh. cat. Forum Barcelona 2004. Barcelona: Lunwerg, 2004.

8   Chase, John, Margaret Crawford and John Kaliski, eds. *Everyday Urbanism.* New York: Monacelli Press, 1999.

9   Zardini, Mirko. "De la ciudad que sube al paisaje que avanza." In *Métropolis, Ciudades, Redes, Paisajes,* edited by Gustavo Gili, Ignasi de Solà-Morales and Xavier Costa. Barcelona: Gustavo Gili, 2005: 208–212.

10   Ábalos, Iñaki and Juan Herreros. "Journey through the Picturesque, a Notebook." In *Landscape Urbanism,* edited by Mostafavi and Najle: 56.

11   See Joachim Krausse and Claude Lichtenstein, eds. *Your Private Sky – R. Buckminster Fuller. Design als Kunst einer Wissenschaft.* Baden: Lars Müller, 1999, and *Your Private Sky: Discourse, R. Buckminster Fuller.* Baden: Lars Müller and Museum of Design, Zürich, 2001. On Superstudio, see Emilio Ambasz, ed. *Italy, The New Domestic Landscape: Achievements and Problems of Italian Design,* exh. cat. New York: Museum of Modern Art & Florence: Centro Di, 1972.

12   Price, Cedric. *A Lung for Midtown Manhattan.* CCA Competition for the Design of Cities, exhibition publication. Montreal: Canadian Centre for Architecture, 2000.

13   Cullen, Gordon. *Townscape.* London: Architectural Press, 1961.

14   Sorkin, Michael, ed. *Variations on a Theme Park: The New American City and the End of Public Space.* New York: Hill and Wang, 1992.

15   Flusty, Steven. "Building Paranoia." In *Architecture of Fear,* edited by Nan Ellin. New York: Princeton Architectural Press, 1997: 47–59.

16   Bauman, Zygmunt. "Living with Foreigners." Address to the conference *Trust and Fear in the City,* Unidea, Unicredit Foundation, Società Umanitaria, Milan, March 30, 2004, proceedings published as *Fiducia e paura nella città.* Milan: Bruno Mondadori, 2005: 33; translation from the Italian by the author.

17   Baumann. "Living with Foreigners": 35.

18   Jacobs, Jane. *The Death and Life of Great American Cities.* New York: Modern Library, 1962.

19   Whyte, William H. *City: Rediscovering the Center.* New York: Doubleday, 1988.

20   Florentine humanist Leonardo Bruni, chancellor of the republic from 1427, wrote his *Laudatio florentinae urbis* in conscious imitation of a 2nd century AD panegyric on Athens. The first Renaissance writer to utilize an ancient literary model for a contemporary text, Bruni nonetheless departs in crucial ways from the Greek model, describing the architecture and character of the city in wholly new terms; published in English trans. by Benjamin G. Kohl, in *From Petrarch to Leonardo Bruni: Studies in Humanistic and Political Literature,* edited by Hans Baron. Chicago: Published by the Newberry Library for the University of Chicago Press, 1968: 232–263.

21   For an analysis of the relationship between the city and the human body, see Richard Sennett. *Flesh and Stone: The Body and the City in Western Civilization.* New York: W. W. Norton, 1994.

22   El-Khoury, Rodolphe. "Polish and Deodorize: Paving the City in Late-Eighteenth-Century France." In *Assemblage,* December, 1996: 6–15.

23   It is worth recalling the Futurists' appreciation for the new noises of the modern city. See Luigi Russolo. *L'arte dei rumori: manifesto futurista.* Milan: Direzione del movimento futurista, March 11, 1913; Milan: Edizioni Futuriste di Poesia, 1916; published in English as *The Art of Noises,* trans. and intro. Barclay Brown. New York: Pendragon Press, 1986.

24   Illich, Ivan. H_2O *and the Waters of Forgetfulness.* London: Marion Boyars, 1986: 49–50.

25   Siegfried, André. "La Geographie des odeurs." Lecture delivered in Paris in 1947, published in *Geographie des odeurs,* edited by Robert Dulau and Jean-Robert Pitte. Paris and Montréal: Éditions L'Harmattan, 1998: 19–23. For a history of the perception of smells, see Alain Corbin. *Le miasme et la jonquille. L'odorat et l'imaginaire social.* Paris: Aubier, 1982. For a general approach to the theme, see also his article, "Histoire et anthropologie sensorielle," first published in *Anthropologie et Sociétés* 14/2 (1990), and later in *Les Temps, le désir et l'horreur: Essais sur le dix-neuvième siècle,* Paris: Flammarion, 2000: 228–241, and *Time, Desire, and Horror: Towards a History of the Senses,* trans. Jean Birrell. Cambridge, MA: Polity Press, 1995.

26 A basic introduction to the work of R. Murray Schafer can be found in *The Soundscape: Our Sonic Environment and the Tuning of the World*. Rochester, VT: Destiny Books, 1977. Also of interest is the research into the sonic landscapes conducted by the Laboratoire Cresson at University of Grenoble. Among the publications coming out of this work is Jean-François Augoyard and Henry Torgue. *A l'écoute de l'environnement. Répertoire des effets sonores*. Marseilles: Éditions Parenthèses, 1995.

27 On the subject of sounds, it is very interesting to look at the data provided by R. Murray Schafer on noises perceived as annoying in different cities at the beginning of the 1970s, which is cited in *The Soundscape*, mentioned above.

28 Banham, Reyner. *The Architecture of the Well-Tempered Environment*. Chicago and London: University of Chicago Press, 1969: 40.

29 Bloomer, Kent C. and Charles Moore. *Body, Memory, and Architecture*. New Haven and London: Yale University Press, 1977.

30 Howes, David. "Introduction." In *Empire of the Senses: The Sensual Culture Reader*, edited by David Howes. Oxford and New York: Berg, 2005: 3–4. This is an interesting foray into the sensual revolution that has taken place in the human and social sciences.

31 Peter Eisenman interviewed by Chiara Visentin in Genoa, 2004; now at www.floornature.com.

32 Smithson, Alison and Peter. *Italian Thoughts*, privately published in Sweden, 1993: 62. See also Juhani Pallasmaa. *The Eyes of the Skin: Architecture and the Senses*. London: Academy Editions, 1995, and Steen Eiler Rasmussen. *Experiencing Architecture*. Cambridge, MA: The MIT Press, 1964. A new attempt to tackle the theme in comprehensive fashion can be found in Joy Monice Malnar and Frank Vodvarka. *Sensory Design*. Minneapolis: University of Minnesota Press, 2004. Noteworthy is the fact that a Sensory Trust has been established (www.sensorytrust.org.uk).

33 See Wurman, Richard Saul. *Information Architects*. New York: Graphis Press, 1996.

34 Nesbitt, Keith V. "Modelling the Multi-Sensory Design Space." In *Australian Symposium on Information Visualization, Conferences in Research and Practice in Information Technology* 9, edited by Peter Eades and Tim Pattison. Sydney: Australian Computer Society, 2001.

35 *California International Conference on Computer Graphics and Interactive Techniques Archive*. San Diego: SIGGRAPH, 2003.

36 Pine II, B. Joseph and James H. Gilmore. *The Experience Economy: Work is Theatre & Every Business a Stage*. Boston: Harvard Business School Press, 1999.

37 On the subject of the privatization of sensory experiences and the experience economy, see David Howes. "Hyperesthesia, or, the Sensual Logic of Late Capitalism." In *Empire of the Senses*, edited by Howes: 281–303.

38 See the entry for *"carattere"* in *Dizionario critico illustrato delle voci più utili all'architetto moderno*, edited by Luciano Semerani. Venice: Fondazione Angelo Masieri & Faenza: Edizione CELI, 1993, and for "character" in Adrian Forty. *A Vocabulary of Modern Architecture*. London: Thames and Hudson, 2000.

39 Lynch, Kevin. *The Image of the City*. Cambridge, MA: MIT Press, 1960.

40 Norberg-Schulz, Christian. *Genius Loci: Towards a Phenomenology of Architecture*. New York: Rizzoli, 1984, first published in Italian, as *Genius loci: Paesaggio, ambiente, architettura,* trans. Anna Maria Norberg-Schulz. Milan: Electa, 1979.

41 On the use of the term *atmosphere* in architecture and city planning, see *Konstruktion von Atmosphären, Daidalos* 68, 1998.

42 Böhme, Gernot. "Atmosphere as an Aesthetic Concept." In *Daidalos* 68, 1998: 114. See also his *Atmosphäre: Essays zur neuen Ästhetik*. Frankfurt am Main: Suhrkamp, 1995, and *Anmutungen, über das Atmosphärische*. Ostfildern: Edition Tertium, 1998.

43 Knodt, Reinhard. "Atmosphären." In *Ästhetische Korrespondenzen: Denken im technischen Raum*. Stuttgart: Philipp Reclam jun., 1994.

44   Ábalos, Iñaki. "Metamorfosi pittoresca." In *Metamorph, Focus,* catalogue of the 9th International Exhibition of Architecture. Venice: Venice Biennale, 2004: 147. English edition, "Picturesque Metamorphosis." In *Metamorph, Focus, Vectors, Trajectories,* edited by Kurt W. Forster and N. Baltzer. Venice: Marsilio, 2004.

45   Kuma, Kengo. "Gardening vs. Architecture." In *Lotus International* 97, June 1998: 46–49.

46   Kuma. "Gardening vs. Architecture": 49.

47   Kuma. "Gardening vs. Architecture": 49.

48   *Sense of the City. An Alternate Approach to Urbanism,* edited by Mirko Zardini. Montreal: Canadian Centre of Architecture; Zürich: Lars Müller Publishers, 2005.

49   It is worthwhile to reread some of James Hillman's writings on the city. See in particular *City and Soul.* Dallas: Center for Civic Leadership, University of Dallas, 1978.

50   Rykwert, Joseph. *The Seduction of Place: The History and Future of the City,* 2nd ed. New York: Vintage Books, 2002: 159.

51   Mitchell, William J. "The Revenge of Place." In *This is Not Architecture: Media Constructions,* edited by Kester Rattenbury. London and New York: Routledge, 2002: 45–53. In this connection, see also François Ascher. *Métapolis ou l'avenir des villes.* Paris: Éditions Odile Jacob, 1995: 263.

Margarethe Kusenbach

The Go-Along Method[1]

When conducting go-alongs, fieldworkers accompany individual informants on their 'natural' outings, and – through asking questions, listening and observing – actively explore their subjects' stream of experiences and practices as they move through, and interact with, their physical and social environment. A hybrid between participant observation and interviewing, go-alongs carry certain advantages when it comes to exploring the role of place in everyday lived experience. Go-alongs are a more modest, but also a more systematic and outcome-oriented version of 'hanging out' with key informants – an ethnographic practice that is highly recommended in virtually all fieldwork manuals and textbooks. Many reflexive descriptions of what ethnographers do characterize 'hanging out' with informants in a variety of social situations as a key strategy. However, because of their extraordinary commitment to a small number of key informants, ethnographers rarely systematically follow a larger number of subjects into a variety of settings. Studies that build 'hanging out' with many or all informants into the overall research design – as a number of classic and contemporary ethnographies do (e.g. Becker 1961; Hochschild 1989; Duneier 1999) – usually focus on their subjects' personal and professional lives at one or two specific locations, thus necessarily downplaying the significance and meaning of less prominent places and of the spatial practices by which different places are linked together.

The goal of the go-along as a research method is at the same time more limited and more focused than the generic ethnographic practice of 'hanging out'. Go-alongs require that ethnographers take a more active stance towards capturing their informants' actions and interpretations. Researchers who utilize this method seek to establish a coherent set of data by spending a particular yet comparable slice of ordinary time with all of their subjects – thus winning in breadth and variety of their collected materials what might get lost in density and intensity. What makes the go-along technique unique is that ethnographers are able to observe their informants' spatial practices *in situ* while accessing their experiences and interpretations at the same time. While going along with subjects is common in ethnographic research, I am not aware that ethnographers have used go-alongs or equivalent techniques *systematically* in previous qualitative studies of everyday life.[2] In any case, sociologists have not yet fully explored the phenomenological potential of this interesting empirical approach.

For the purpose of authenticity, it is crucial to conduct what I have previously referred to as 'natural' go-alongs. By this I mean go-alongs that follow informants into their familiar environments and track outings they would go on anyway as closely as possible, for instance with respect to the particular day, the time of the day, and the routes of the regular trip. In contrast, 'contrived' or experimental go-alongs – meaning when researchers take informants into unfamiliar territory or engage them in activities that are not part of their own routines – might produce appealing data, but not of the kind that would greatly enhance our understanding of the subjects' authentic practices and interpretations.

Even though 'natural' go-alongs are ideally rooted in informants' everyday routines, this research technique is obviously not a 'naturally occurring' social occasion. It is rather unlikely that informants are accompanied on their routine trips by acquaintances who engage them in discussing their perceptions and interpretations of the physical and social environment. There can be no doubt that go-alongs, like interviews and even participant observation, are always 'contrived' social situations that disturb the unfolding of ordinary events. Go-alongs intentionally aim at capturing the stream of perceptions, emotions and interpretations that informants usually keep to themselves. The presence and curiosity of someone else undoubtedly intrudes upon and alters this delicate, private dimension of lived experience.[3]

I found that conducting go-alongs with more than one person at a time, for instance accompanying a couple walking their dog around the neighborhood or running errands together, can be very productive. The presence of a partner or friend can reduce some of the obvious discomfort that a number of informants feel about being followed in, and queried about, their mundane local practices by an ethnographer. This does not, however, mean that go-alongs with couples are therefore more 'natural' events. They only produce a different kind of artificiality and cannot solve the much more fundamental dilemma of researcher reactivity. Even so: it is still useful to distinguish between the contributions of more and less contrived versions of go-alongs. While they can never be completely 'natural' social situations, and thus always impact the experiences that subjects would have without such company, the less contrived ones stand a much better chance of uncovering

aspects of individual lived experience that frequently remain hidden during participant observations, sit-down interviews and more experimental types of go-alongs.

The most common and practical modes of go-alongs are 'walk alongs' (on foot)
and 'ride-alongs' (on wheels), yet others are certainly possible. Many times, go-alongs
will involve a mixture of activities and the use of more than one mode of transportation. Of the 50 go-alongs that I conducted, three-quarters were walk-alongs and
the rest ride-alongs or mixed types. My go-alongs lasted anywhere from a few minutes (walking with an informant to the gas station on the corner to buy cigarettes)
to many hours (spending almost entire days with informants as they worked, ran
errands and socialized). In my experience, a productive time window for a go-along
is about an hour to 90 minutes.

I experimented with audio-recording go-alongs, taking jottings and photos, and
with not making any records during the actual outing. I found audio-recordings
particularly useful in the case of ride-alongs because of the much faster and more
urgent pace of events, making it difficult to ask informants for clarifications and
to mentally keep track of the sequence of situations. Overall, I found ride-alongs
to be less effective than walk-alongs mainly for these reasons. Jotting down key
phrases and facts on the spot turned out to be quite helpful, as long as it did not
interfere with the original pace or the nature of the outing. In the end, which
strategy of recording go-alongs is most useful depends on the variable comfort level
of informants as well as on the personal preferences of the researcher (Emerson et
al. 1995). What is most important is to expand any records or mental notes into full
sets of descriptive fieldnotes as soon as possible after completing a go-along.

What exactly did I emphasize while conducting go-alongs? I tried giving my informants as little direction as possible with regard to what I would like them to talk
about. If they insisted on instructions, I asked them to comment on whatever came
to mind while looking at and moving through places and also to share with me what
they usually experienced during routine trips. On occasion, I pointed to a nearby
feature in the environment that was difficult to overlook and asked my subjects
what they thought of, or felt about, this particular object in order to demonstrate
what kind of information I was looking for. Even though the telling of my informants' experiences was sporadically invoked by my presence, I avoided participat-
ing in the selection or the contents of their narratives. In any case, I could have
never anticipated which places and environmental features stood out in their minds
and how they perceived and interpreted them.

In sum, the strengths and advantages of participant observation, interviewing and go-alongs accumulate when they are pursued in combination. The argument here is not one of superiority but for becoming more self-conscious about expanding the range of data-gathering techniques in order to exploit the different perspectives and angles each provides. As Becker (1958: 657) points out, social scientists should not only strive to collect many instances of an identified phenomenon but also seek to gather 'many kinds of evidence' to enhance the validity of a particular conclusion.[4]

At the very least, including systematic yet subject-driven go-alongs into the research design of an ethnographic study will provide fieldworkers with the opportunity to schedule multiple returns to subjects who might be hesitant to make themselves available for a formal follow-up interview. Furthermore, go-alongs create excellent opportunities to conduct 'unobserved' observations of social settings and situations that happen to be sensitive to unaccompanied outsiders. Ultimately, go-alongs can do more than merely enhance field access and contacts.

Notes

1   Editorial note: The following remarks on the go-along method are an extract from Kusenbach's essay 'Street Phenomenology: The Go-Along as Ethnographic Research Tool.' In *Ethnography* vol. 4, 3, 2003. They provide a methodological background for the following chapter by Loïc Wacquant, who conducts a 'ride-along' during his field research.

2   There are always exceptions. In 1959, Lynch and Rivkin claimed to have conducted the first study 'where respondents have been recorded while actually moving through the city itself' (Lynch and Rivkin 1970: 631). This is in fact not quite correct. The researchers sent 20 subjects – some of them familiar with the area, others not – on a walk around an urban block in Boston and questioned them *afterwards* about what they experienced. Lynch and Rivkin are aware that this technique 'intensifies, and possibly distorts the usual day-by-day perception of the city' but still assert that it has advantages over other approaches. Katz (1999) employs a variety of ethnographic methods to capture the lived experience of emotions. One chapter discussing road rage is based on student interviews with Los Angeles drivers, quite a number of them conducted *while driving*. This gave the student interviewers the opportunity to triangulate what they learned from their subjects about vehicular behavior with their own observations. See also Patricia Paperman's article on the uniform as an interaction device (Paperman 2003), where she notes that it was only when she accompanied a third team of subway police that she could access their work in process.

3   Over the course of the research on two urban neighborhoods (as reported in Kusenbach's essay "Street Phenomenology"; AS), as I learned many intimate details about the lives of my informants, I had to monitor myself carefully not to use this vast stock of knowledge as a conversational resource in developing bonds with new or difficult informants. Some realized that I knew a lot and were eager

to find out intimate details about their neighbors and I had to consciously resist the tendency to share such information. Because I did not act in accordance with the rules of casual conversations, go-alongs were not quite like chats that could have occurred between neighbors. Yet they were neither very formal nor problematic encounters, even though some informants were obviously less comfortable discussing their experiences and practices with me than others.

4   Goffman's famous remarks on how to conduct fieldwork seem to suggest a similar point. He was recorded saying: '[Jackie] takes seriously what people say. I don't give hardly any weight to what people say, but I try to triangulate what they're saying with events' (Goffman 1989: 131).

References

Becker, Howard S. 'Problems of Inference and Proof in Participant Observation.' In *American Sociological Review* 23, 1958: 652–60.

Becker, Howard S. *Boys in White: Student Culture in Medical School.* New Brunswick, NJ: Transaction Books, 1961.

Certeau, Michel de. 'Practices of Space.' In *On Signs,* edited by Marshall Blonsky. Baltimore, MD: Johns Hopkins University Press, 1984.

Duneier, Mitchell. *Sidewalk.* New York: Farrar, Straus & Giroux, 1999.

Emerson, Robert M., Rachel I. Fretz and Linda L. Shaw. *Writing Ethnographic Fieldnotes.* Chicago: University of Chicago Press, 1995.

Goffman, Erving. *Behavior in Public Places: Notes on the Social Organization of Gatherings.* New York: Free Press, 1963.

Goffman, Erving. *Frame Analysis: An Essay on the Organization of Experience.* New York: Harper & Row, 1974.

Goffman, Erving. 'The Interaction Order.' In *American Sociological Review* 48, 1983: 1–17.

Granovetter, Mark S. 'The Strength of Weak Ties.' In *American Journal of Sociology* 78(6)1973: 1360–80.

Kusenbach, Margarethe. *Neighboring: An Ethnographic Study of Community in Urban Hollywood.* Dissertation. University of California, Los Angeles, 2003.

Leder, Drew. *The Absent Body.* Chicago: University of Chicago Press, 1990.

Lofland, Lyn H. *The Public Realm.* New York: De Gruyter, 1998.

Milligan, Melinda J. 'Interactional Past and potential: The Social Construction of Place Attachment.' In *Symbolic Interaction* 21, 1998: 1–33.

Paperman, Patricia. 'Surveillance Underground. The Uniform as an Interaction Device.' In *Ethnography,* vol. 4, 3, 2003: 397-419.

Schutz, Alfred. *Reflections on the Problem of Relevance.* New Haven, CT: Yale University Press, 1970.

Seamon, David. *A Geography of the Lifeworld.* New York: St Martin's Press, 1979.

NELE BRÖNNER

Loïc Wacquant

Urban Desolation and Symbolic Denigration in the Hyperghetto

Curtis and I set the electronic alarm on and promptly exit through the gym's front door, scurrying straight into his Jeep Comanche lest the bitter cold air seize and smother us. In the yellowish glare of the wintry street lights, I watch coach DeeDee calmly go through his nightly routine: with sur-geon-like gestures at once precise and economical, he draws the rusty metal grate shut, tugs the heavy chain through its twisted and tangled bars, and closes the padlock with a deft snap of the wrist. (When I ask him to let me handle the gym's gate to relieve the strain on his arthritic hands, his typical reply is: "No, I know how to do it faster 'n anybody. I know this fence: I locked it a million times").

Old Floyd has offered to take DeeDee home tonight, as he does every now and again when he get overly anxious to press the venerable coach about the (ever-so remote) possibility of him "turn-ing pro" at some point down the road. DeeDee haltingly folds his largish hulk of a body into the small brown Toyota, his grocery paper bag between his long legs, knees up nearly rubbing against his stout chin. He waves at me gently and I read on his grinning lips, "See you tomorrow brother Louie."

Curtis insists on taking me to his neighborhood church for a visit with his pastor. As we hun-ker down inside his four-wheeler, he flips on a tape by the rap band, No More Colors, full tilt and the heavily distorted sound floods the cabin with its frenetic, pulsating rhythm. "It's my fav'rite song, 'cause it's positive: it tell d'kids enough killin's an' dope and shootin' an' stuff, don't do dat 'cause 'We're All Blacks, We're All in the Same Gang'!" – the song's inspiring if raucous chorus. He peevedly thumps on the dashboard to try and get the speaker on the driver's side to function and settles straight up into his leather seat. And then the morbid spectacle of the corridor of dere-liction that is 63rd Street flashes by us as we rush towards Stony Island Avenue under the rusty elevated train line.

Curtis: At one time this neighbo'hood, you could get *anythin'* up and down this neighbo'hoo' – I mean, this was like d'*downtown* for the Southeast side. I mean, (enthusiastic) you talkin' 'bout Buster Browns, uh McDonald's, Burger King, uh, Kenny Shoes, P's, I mean, I mean: *you name it,* you can get it up-n'-down here. Jus',

I mean dis use to be a *hot spot* right back, back in the sixties, da late or early sixties. Yeah, dis used to be the spot right here.

Louie: What is it like today?

Today i's *down*. I mean, lotta thin's is changed. You can see fo' yo'self that everythin' is, (shaking his head) *half offa d'buildin's aroun' here is boarded up.*

What kindsa things go on in the street right here on 63rd Street?

Well, you have a lotta street walkers, you have yo' gang-bangers, you have yo' *dope dealers,* yo' *dope users* – I mean (a tad defensive) that's in every neighbo'hoo', I'm not jus' sayin' this neighbo'hoo'. I mean you have dat around here.

And it's *bad for the kids* that's comin' up in the neighbo'hoo' 'cause that's who they have to look up. They got people like *dese guys* (gesturing towards a cluster of men "shooting the breeze" by the entrance of a liquor store) tha's doin' *everythin' wrong* to look up to. I mean! Is that anythin' to try t'teach a kid, to be a dope dealer or a dope user, or to be a pimp?

You see like guys like this *hangin' out* up on d'street, *jus'* bein' aroun', *jus' hangin'* around bummin' for quarters 'n' dimes and stuff t'buy 'em wine. (Censoriously) It's *bad* ya know, that dese guys, they messed up they lives and stuff, ya know, or they don't *care* too much about you know, how dey life gonna turn out to be. Ya know, half-a 'em is in they late forties, late thirties and jus' don't care anymore, but it's *bad* dat we got dese guys out here like this jus' for d'kids to look up to.

People that don't know nuttin' about the Southeast side, comin' 'roun' here and see this, and the first thin' they think about (mockingly, in an exaggeratedly scared voice) *"aw'! I'm not getting' out ma car!* I'm not gon' leave ma car. I don't want ma kids to be 'round here or anythin'" ya know. *But,* it's somethin' for 'em to do. (He honks a blue Cadillac snailing along in front of us). You see everythin' is boarded up. They tryin' to put a washer and dryer over here (he points to an abandoned building), a laundromat over here. Now thata be good for the neighbo'hoo', for the community.

And look over here on the left…

It's a store that sell liquor, with another store that's boarded up that useta sell liquor an', you see people walkin' up an' down d'street with jus', they on a wish an' a prayer…

Ya know, *you can never say what's on dese guys min'*, what's on d'peoples min' out dere, ya know: *they out here ta live, they live day-by-day.* And you know (raucous) *it's baaad,* jus' –

jus' *imagine* you not havin' *a dream,* or anythin' that you tryin' *t'accomplish outa life* and (his pace accelerating) you *wake up,* an' you got yo' fingers crossed hopin' that one of yo' frien's, or somebody dat you know come in knock on yo' door an' you come outside and see 'em and they got a *scheme* up. (in a passionate, revolted, voice) I mean ya know you have ta *live like that everyday!*

To hope that somebody come an' tell you dat they gotta, they got a *money idea* to make you, give ya a coupla dollars or som'thin' jus' go get drunk or le's go buy some dope and *get high?* I mean, ya know, (his tone turning scared) I mean, could you *IMAGINE livin' a life like that?*

Now, I have seen a lotta ma frien's an' stuff, lotta guys that I be grew up with, a lotta guys that, ya know, tha's been, tha's been of age before I have, I see a lotta 'em *use drugs* n' *deal drugs* and did various thin's to, ya know, try ta fix they habit. Get theyself, you know, some dope, or put some money in they pocket ta try t'take care of theyself.

I know that's the life that they wanted to live but *I choose* the opposite. (his delivery speeds up, as if he was scared again at the mere thought of the possibility) I couldn't, ya know, it's a headache – couldn't wake up, *I couldn't see myself wakin' up ev'ry day* an' stuff, wakin' up and *hopin'* that I find somebody ta, ya know, somebody tha's got a money idea ta help me get some money or put some money in ma pocket for me and my kids.

The guys that you grew up with, what've they become?

Ya know, my mom told me when I was of age an' stuff, I think aroun' 'bout fourteen or fifteen, she say it's gonna be a time when you gonna see a lotta yo' frien's, some o'them gonna die an' some o' them gonna go to jail. N' *sho' enough* I seen 'em, a lotta 'em, 'bout half o'them – well, not half, that'd be stretchin' it a lil' bit too much, but a lotta ma friends has passed away: *gang-bangin'* or a lotta 'em sellin' dope, I have a lotta frien's jus' *sellin',* jus' dealin' dope, (his voice rising, not indignant but outraged) *strung out on dope, sellin' cocaine* jus' to do another typa dope, uh – they call it Karachi I think, tha's a downer.

(voice fading) N' a lotta my frien's is in jail. Some o'my frien's, I mean, I can count d'friends on my own *one hand that did finish school* and ya know, pursue they career in uh ya know, bus'ness career uh, ya know, tha's jus' tryin' to make somethin' out theyself. I can count 'em on one hand. But I still see 'em, ya know, and speak to 'em...

(Woodlawn field notebooks, 17 October 1990)

The scene of urban desolation and social despair etched in this conversation and captured by the picture of 63rd Street, one of the ghostly thoroughfares transecting Chicago's collapsing black ghetto at century's close, invites us to reflect on the link between the built environment, social structure, and collective psychology. More precisely, it points to the need to elaborate theoretically and empirically the connections between urban desolation and symbolic denigration in America's racialized urban core and assorted territories of relegation in the dualizing metropolis of the advanced societies (Wacquant 2008): how the daily experience of material dilapidation, ethno-racial seclusion and socioeconomic marginality translates into the corrosion of the self, the rasping of interpersonal ties, and the skewing of public policy through the mediation of sulfurous cognition fastened onto a defamed place.

The link between ecology, morphology and representations was a theme central to the Durkheimian school of sociology, as attested by such tomes as Emile Durkheim's ([1912] 1995) celebrated analysis of "collective effervescence" in *The Elementary Forms of Religious Life,* Marcel Mauss's bold investigation of *Seasonal Variations of the Eskimo* (Mauss and Beuchat [1906] 1979), and Maurice Halbwachs's ([1942] 1958) probing *Psychology of Social Class;* but it has rarely been addressed frontally by students of urban inequality and poverty. From Robert Park and Ernest Burgess to Louis Wirth on down to his post-war students, the Chicago school did posit a correspondence between metropolitan morphology and psychology, with distinct "moral regions" corresponding roughly to the evolving ethnic and class quartering of space in the American city (Hannerz 1980). But its exponents were so intent on fighting the deep anti-urbanism of America's national culture and on elaborating the notion of (sub)cultural diversity that they devoted little attention to the negative synergy between material deterioration, institutional devolution, and the mental atmosphere of neighborhoods, in spite of the explosive racial tensions and conflictive class transformation roiling the metropolis under their eyes. More problematic still, they were oblivious to the role of the state as a stratifying and classifying agency that wields a dominant influence on the social and symbolic order of the city.

Likewise, the classic studies of the crisis of the dark ghetto during and after the upheavals of the 1960s addressed collective deprecation and depression, but they linked them primarily to pervasive unemployment and continued racial discrimination inflicted upon lower-class blacks (Clark 1965; Liebow 1967; Rainwater 1970;

Glasgow 1980; Wilson 1987), rather than to their proximate socio-spatial milieu and its distinctive ambiance and image. In this regard, they converged with the resurgent Marxist and political-economic approaches to urban disparity, which typically treated collective representations as secondary efflorescence or reflexes of material forces rooted in the realm of production and its disjuncture from the world of "community" (Katznelson 1981; Harvey 1989; Walton 1993). By the 1990s, the academic tale of the "underclass" took it as axiomatic that the inner-city poor were both destitute and dispirited – indeed, in the hegemonic accounts, the moral degradation of this segment of the urban proletariat was not a consequence but the cause of their predicament. But it neither documented nor related this state of mind to the physical and social state of the crumbling ghetto and their structural determinants. With few partial and oblique exceptions (e.g., Bourdieu et al. [1993] 1999; Snow and Anderson 1993; Bourgois 1995; Young 2004; Gay 2005; Jamoulle 2008), then, observers of landscapes of urban dereliction have paid little attention to the symbolic valence and psychological tenor of entrapment at the bottom of the hierarchy of places that make up the city. This essay is an invitation to fill this gap.

The barren and brutal scenery featured you can see in the image on page 168 is located in Woodlawn, barely two hundred yards from the University of Chicago Law School, but worlds away from it as it were, and a few blocks east of the boxing gym that served as hub for the ethnographic component of two nested studies, the one a carnal anthropology of prizefighting as plebeian bodily craft carried out in 1988–1991, and the other a comparative sociology of the dynamics and experience of urban marginality in the black American ghetto and the urban periphery of Western Europe stretched over the ensuing decade (Wacquant 2004, 2008). It gives a glimpse of the *physical dilapidation, social decay and stunning depopulation* that were the first palpable features of everyday life in the American hyperghetto at century's close. Between 1950 and 1990, the ranks of Woodlawnites sank from 81,300 to a mere 27,500 as their ethnic composition swung from 62% white to 98% black.[1] The number of housing units plummeted apace, from 29,616 to 13,109, with fully one-fifth of the remaining structures left vacant, due to waves of building abandonment, arson, and demolition. As the wage labor market and the welfare state both retrenched from the area in the wake of the rageful riots of 1968 in response to the assassination of Martin Luther King, economic involution and organizational desertification set in. The decline and death of hundreds of commercial, social and cultural establishments, from machine shops and barber shops, to hotels and brothels, theaters and restaurants, churches and banks, clothing outlets and day-care centers, turned a vibrant neighborhood into an urban wasteland doubly segregated by race and class. The bustling commercial artery of 63rd Street mutated into a lugubrious strip dotted with the burnt-out carcasses of stores, boarded-up buildings (scavenged for metal, fixtures, and bricks), and vacant lots strewn with weeds, broken glass, and garbage.[2] Extending the thrust of the "New federalism" dictated by Washington after 1980, city policy skirted away from supporting lower-class residents and districts toward attracting corporations and beefing up middle-class amenities. The ensuing breakdown of public services in the metropolitan core undermined the local institutions central to the strategies of preservation of the urban poor (Sánchez-Jankowski 2008), leaving them mired in rampant joblessness, crushing poverty and escalating crime, as the predatory commerce of the street grew to fill the vacuum left by the ebbing of the formal economy.

How did the racially skewed economic, demographic, and political forces that combined to gut out the erstwhile proud Black Metropolis of Chicago (Drake and Cayton [1945], 1963), leaving it in a state of infrastructural and institutional abandonment unknown and unthinkable in Western European cities (see Kazepov 2005 for comparison), impress the consciousness of its residents? Curtis's depiction of 63rd Street indicates how urban desolation translates into *collective demoralization,* registered in feelings of dejection, dread, and anger, as well as in the inordinately high rates of malnutrition and obesity (attested by the advertisement for "The Big Fish"), alcoholism and drug abuse, depression and assorted mental afflictions detected in the hyperghetto. The material crumbling of the neighborhood is but the physical manifestation of the sudden closure of the opportunity structure, incarnated by the social phantoms roving the street for whom existence is reduced to sheer subsistence *("they out here ta live, they live day-by-day").* The amputation of objective life chances, in turn, collapses the social horizon of subjective expectations, leaving little room between utter despair ("jus' *imagine* you not havin' *a dream*") and oneirism, represented, on the legal side, by massive participation in the Illinois state lottery and, on the illegal side, by narcotics' distribution and consumption.

Anthropologists of place have taught us that public space is pregnant with civic meaning (Low and Smith 2006). In this regard, the physical disrepair and institutional dilapidation of the neighborhood cannot but generate an abiding *sense of social inferiority* by communicating to its residents that they are second- or third-class

Urban desolation on 61st Street near Kimbark
Avenue, South Side of Chicago
© Loïc Wacquant

citizens undeserving of the attention of city officials and of the care of its agencies. This message of social worthlessness is conveyed not only by the crumbling bridges, broken sidewalks, leaking sewers, and by the corrugated hulk of the elevated train line that would get dismantled a few years later, but also by the gradual replacement of the social welfare treatment of marginality by its punitive management through the aggressive rolling out of the police, the courts, and the prison in and around the hyperghetto, leading to astronomical rates of incarceration for lower-class blacks (Wacquant 2009). It is reinforced by the distinctive advertising imagery that visually dominates the streets. Billboards invite passers-by to seek succor in the embrace of hard liquor ("Vampin' with the Brothers: Colt 45," "Misbehavin': Canadian Mist," "Be Cool: Smirnoff Vodka"); they remind them of their present economic quandary and of the dreary fate awaiting their children ("Get A Job – Call Now – 19 dollars"; "No School, No Future"); and they invite them to resolve on their own festering problems that should be the responsibility of government ("Stop Black On Black Crime") or yet to collaborate with its repressive arm ("Save A Life: Tell On Your Neighborhood Drug Dealer").

The ominous placard blaring "Addiction is Slavery" over a black hand clutching drug pills reactivates the historic dishonor of servitude and links it syntagmatically with urban dispossession – except to suggest that today's inner-city derelicts are to blame for their own predicament, insofar as their bondage is portrayed as the product, not of subordination to a (white) master abetted by an indifferent political machinery, but of a relation of self to self, in keeping with the neoliberal trope of individual responsibility that has percolated down to the rock bottom of the social order (as when Curtis seeks to establish his civic *bona fides* by exclaiming about the street zombies caught in the vortex of drugs and despair: "That's the life that they wanted to live but *I choose* the opposite"). Indeed, both whites and the state are the *absent presence* that haunts the picture by their joint empirical invisibility and causal liability.

The decrepit physical setting, the unchecked institutional dysfunction, the grinding demoralization and the pervasive aura of collective indignity suffusing the hyperghetto combine to tag its residents with an "undesired differentness" whose "discrediting effect is very extensive" (Goffman 1963: 5, 3), that is, a *stigma attached to territory* which becomes superimposed onto and redoubles the stigmata of race and poverty. People trapped in districts of social perdition widely perceived as urban warts, nests of vice and violence where only the discards of society would brook living, respond to the taint associated with dwelling in the *regio non grata* of their metropolis by deploying four strategies of symbolic self-protection.[3] The first is *mutual distancing and the elaboration of micro-differences:* they disavow knowing people around them and stress whatever minor personal property can establish separation from a population and a place they know to be defiled and defiling. The second strategy is *lateral denigration,* which consists in adopting the vituperative representations held by outsiders and in applying these to one's neighbors, effectively relaying and reverberating the scornful gaze society trains onto its urban outcasts ("dese guys, they messed up they lives or they don't *care* too much about dey life gonna turn out to be"). A third reaction to spatial vilification is to *retreat into the private sphere* and seek refuge in the restricted social and moral economy of the household, while a fourth is to *exit the neighborhood* as soon as one garners the resources needed to depart (as attested by the outmigration that cut the population of Woodlawn by 30% in the 1980s alone).[4]

Territorial degradation and defamation exercise a deleterious influence on the social structure of urban marginality through two routes. First, internally, stigmatization feeds back into demoralization, and the two converge to encourage residents of districts of dereliction to disassociate themselves from their neighbors, shrinking their networks and restricting their joint activities. This social withdrawal and symbolic disidentification, in turn, undermine local cohesion, hamper collective mobilization, and help generate the very atomism that the dominant discourse on zones of urban dispossession claims is one of their inherent features. Second, on the external front, spatial stigma alters the perception and skews the judgements and actions of the surrounding citizenry, commercial operators, and government officials.[5] Outsiders fear coming into the neighborhood and commonly impute a wide range of nefarious traits to its inhabitants. Businesses are reticent to open facilities or to provide services for customers in "no-go areas." Employers hesitate to hire job applicants who, coming from them, are unreflectively suspected of having a lax work ethic and lower moral standards, leading to pervasive *address discrimination*. Most decisively, when urban degradation and symbolic devaluation intensify to the point where neighborhoods of relegation appear to be beyond salvage, they provide political leaders and state bureaucrats with warrants for deploying aggressive policies of containment, discipline and dispersal that further disorganize the urban poor under the pretext of improving their opportunities – as witnessed, for instance, by the campaign of "deconcentration" of public housing launched in the United States in the 1990s (Crump 2002) and the kindred policy of destruction of large clusters of low-income estates now under way across Western Europe (Musterd and Andersson 2005) that propose a false spatial solution to the real economic and political problems destabilizing lower-class districts.

This essay has proposed that the social psychology of place operates in the manner of a symbolic cog latching the macro-determinants of urban political economy to the life options and strategies of the poor at ground level through the mediation of the negative collective representations of dispossessed districts that come to be shared by their inhabitants, by city dwellers around them, and by the political and administrative elites which design and run the range of public policies and services aimed at deprived populations. This points to the need for detailed field studies tracking how the stigma fastened on neighborhoods of relegation across advanced Western societies – the hyperghetto in the United States, the degraded working-class *banlieues* in France, the sink estates in the United Kingdom, the *krottenwijk* in the Netherlands, etc. – twists the nexus of urban ecology, morphology, and psychology and thereby skews the functioning of the institutions that shape the destiny of urban outcasts in the era of rising social insecurity.[6]

Notes

1   All the figures in this section are culled and computed from various tables and appendices in Chicago Fact Book Consortium (1995), which itself relies on geocoded tabulations of tract-level data from the 1990 Census.

2   This is not a Chicago particularity, as documented by Vergara's (2003) stunning photographic collage on the ghostly ruins of the inner cities of New York City, Newark and Camden (New Jersey), Philadelphia, Baltimore, Gary (Indiana), Detroit and Los Angeles.

3   See Wacquant (2007) for a discussion of the specificities of territorial stigma – by contraposition to what Erving Goffman characterizes as physical, moral, and tribal stigmata – and of the thorny dilemmas it creates for collective claims-making and group formation among the urban precariat.

4   This is only a temporary or apparent solution: subproletarian families who leave their run-down districts in the American city do not go very far in social and physical space. They typically relocate in an adjacent area or in another tract sporting similar ecological, economic, and demographic properties (Sharkey 2008).

5   "We believe that the person with a stigma is not quite human. On this assumption, we exercise a variety of discriminations, through which we effectively, if often unthinkingly, reduce his life chances. We construct a stigma-theory, an ideology to explain his inferiority and to account for the danger he represents" (Goffman 1963: 5).

6   See the multidisciplinary investigations of the roots, forms, and effects of territorial taint in eight countries on three continents gathered in Slater, Pereira and Wacquant (2014).

References

Bourgois, Philippe. *In Search of Respect: Selling Crack in El Barrio*. New York: Cambridge University Press, 1995.

Bourdieu, Pierre et al. *The Weight of the World: Social Suffering in Contemporary Society*. Cambridge: Polity Press, (1993) 1999.

Chicago Fact Book Consortium. *Local Community Fact Book. Chicago Metropolitan Area*. Chicago: Academy Chicago Publishers, 1995.

Clark, Kenneth B. *Dark Ghetto: Dilemmas of Social Power*. New York: Harper, 1965.

Crump, Jeff. "Deconcentration by Demolition: Public Housing, Poverty, and Urban Policy." In *Environment and Planning D: Society and Space* 20, no. 5, 2002: 581–96.

Drake, St. Clair and Horace R. Cayton. *Black Metropolis: A Study of Negro Life in a Northern City*. Chicago: University of Chicago Press (1945), new ed. 1993.

Durkheim, Emile. *The Elementary Forms of Religious Life*. Trans. and with an introduction by Karen E. Fields. New York: Free Press (1912), 1995.

Gay, Robert. *Lucia: Testimonies of a Brazilian Drug Dealer's Woman*. Philadelphia: Temple University Press, 2005.

Glasgow, Douglas G. *The Black Underclass: Poverty, Unemployment, and the Entrapment of Ghetto Youth*. New York: Vintage, 1980.

Goffman, Erving. *Stigma: Notes on the Management of Spoiled Identity*. New York: Simon and Schuster, 1963.

Halbwachs, Maurice. *The Psychology of Social Class*. London: Heinemann (1942), 1958.

Hannerz, Ulf. *Exploring the City: Inquiries Toward an Urban Anthropology*. New York: Columbia University Press, 1980.

Harvey, David. *The Urban Experience*. Baltimore: The Johns Hopkins University Press, 1989.

Jamoulle, Pascale. *Des hommes sur le fil. La construction de l'identité masculine en milieux précaires*. Paris: La Découverte, 2008.

Kazepov, Yuri, ed. *Cities of Europe: Changing Contexts. Local Arrangement and the Challenge to Urban Cohesion.* Cambridge, UK: Wiley-Blackwell, 2005.

Katznelson, Ira. *City Trenches: Urban Politics and the Patterning of Class in the United States.* New York: Pantheon, 1981.

Liebow, Elliot. *Tally's Corner: A Study of Negro Streetcorner Men.* Addison: Rowman & Littlefield (1967), new ed. 2003.

Low, Setha and Neil Smith, eds. *The Politics of Public Space.* New York: Routledge, 2006.

Mauss, Marcel and Henri Beuchat. *Seasonal Variations of the Eskimo: A Study in Social Morphology.* London: Routledge & Kegan Paul (1906), 1979.

Musterd, Sako and Roger Andersson. "Housing Mix, Social Mix, and Social Opportunities." In *Urban Affairs Review* 40, no. 6, 2005: 761–790.

Rainwater, Lee. *Behind Ghetto Walls: Black Families in a Federal Slum.* Chicago: Aldine Publishing Company, 1970.

Sánchez-Jankowski, Martin. *Cracks in the Pavement: Social Change and Resilience in Poor Neighborhoods.* Berkeley: University of California Press, 2008.

Sharkey, Patrick. "The Intergenerational Transmission of Context." In *American Journal of Sociology* 113, no. 4 (December), 2008: 931–969.

Slater, Tom, Virgílio Pereira and Loïc Wacquant (eds.). Special issue of *Environment & Planning A* on "Territorial Stigmatization," vol. 46, no. 6, 2014.

Snow, David A. and Leon Anderson. *Down on Their Luck: A Study of Homeless Street People.* Berkeley: University of California Press, 1993.

Vergara, Camilo. *American Ruins.* New York: Monacelli, 2003.

Wacquant, Loïc. *Body and Soul: Notebooks of An Apprentice Boxer.* New York: Oxford University Press, (2000), 2004.

Wacquant, Loïc. "Territorial Stigmatization in the Age of Advanced Marginality." In *Thesis Eleven* 91 (November), 2007: 66–77.

Wacquant, Loïc. *Urban Outcasts: A Comparative Sociology of Advanced Marginality.* Cambridge, UK: Polity Press, 2008.

Wacquant, Loïc. *Punishing the Poor: The Neoliberal Government of Social Insecurity.* Durham and London: Duke University Press, 2009.

Walton, John. "Urban Sociology: The Contribution and Limits of Political Economy." In *Annual Review of Sociology* 19, 1993: 301–320.

Wilson, William Julius. *The Truly Disadvantaged: The Inner City, the Underclass, and Public Policy.* Chicago: University of Chicago Press, 1987.

Young, Alford A., Jr. *The Minds of Marginalized Black Men: Making Sense of Mobility, Opportunity and Future Life Chances.* Princeton: Princeton University Press, 2004.

Epilogue

Orvar Löfgren

Doing an Ethnography of "Non-Events"[1]

When we started working on this project some years ago we were certain about only one thing. We wanted to find ways of doing a cultural analysis of the non-eventful and inconspicuous – of transit spaces, in-between times, pauses, and moments of indecision. In particular, we wanted to write about imagination. But where to start? And what kind of methodology should we use?

Looking back on the research, we would like to focus not so much on theoretical inspirations but on the everyday life of the project, when we searched for ideas and approaches and experimented with methods and materials.

Stumbling Along?

In the secure world of research handbooks a study proceeds in well-planned steps, driven by clear ideas about aims, materials, and methods. In cultural analysis the process tends to be messier, and this book is no exception. When in the end we asked ourselves how we had carried out the research, we found the process difficult to reconstruct. Although our book may give the impression of intentional research, the fact is that many of the choices and decisions that determined the final text are concealed even from us.

Yet we think it is important to try to clarify our work, not least because for some years now there have been pleas for celebrating such unsystematic dimensions of research as aimless rambling and random reading. This trend is encapsulated in the buzzword serendipity, the art of not knowing what you are looking for, and the celebration of creative wild thinking. Yet such labels conceal the cumulative and systematic dimensions of even seemingly anarchistic analytical work.

The research process may be experienced as stumbling along winding paths full of detours, dead ends, and chance encounters. Still, one has to make decisions about when to turn, stop, or go back, and about choosing among questions, materials, and perspectives. Such "messy" research methods therefore need to be described, not to establish recipes for "how to do cultural analysis" but to understand what actually happens in the course of a project. How did we develop the search, what did we do when we got stuck or felt lost, how did we mix materials and ideas, and what did constant rewriting do to the analysis?

Compared with much of our earlier ethnological studies, which were based on fieldwork and interviews in specific communities or groups, or historical studies using better-known kinds of source material, this project turned out to be much more disorganized, and the goal kept changing. Thanks to the archaeological remains in our computers of early outlines, drafts, and versions of this book, reconstruction is – to some extent – possible. Moreover, the present book has a forerunner in our Swedish book of 2007, and we found it enlightening to compare the two texts, which are quite different.

Creating Arenas

From the beginning we thought about the role of imagination in everyday life. Later we narrowed this down to daydreaming. When we looked for an analytical perspective in the literature, we found it to be mainly psychological, focusing on individuals and on the contents, forms, meanings, and functions of daydreams. Why do people daydream, how can their dreams be interpreted? Our first versions of this text were about different kinds of fantasies and their contents, based partly upon the literature available, as well as upon introspection and conversations with others.

Normally the next step would have been to go out and conduct interviews, asking people about their fantasies. But something held us back. We felt that it might be difficult and unproductive to head straight for that target. Even if they were, contrary to our expectations, to tell us about their private daydreams, what would we do with these stories other than proceed in the psychological tradition? But we wanted our analysis to focus more on the cultural.

One way to accomplish this was to stop thinking about the whys of day dreaming and instead ask how. In what situations does daydreaming occur, what kinds of props and materials are used in this elusive activity? It was at this stage that we stopped thinking of daydreaming as a mental activity and instead began to look for the situations and material conditions in which it takes place. This led us into the arenas of waiting and routines, two of the platforms for daydreaming.

Waiting turned out to be productive territory for the imagination because people often are (or seem to be) mentally absent while waiting. In the same way, mindless routines offer a chance to daydream. Studying these platforms and stages of daydreaming allowed us to approach the intangible reality of imagination in a more down-to-earth way – not something we had grasped or planned when we set off on this project.

We also didn't know exactly how to handle the three different versions of "doing nothing." It was not initially our intention to discuss waiting through the lens of various dissimilar cases (petrol queues in Nigeria, train stations in England, and prenatal clinics in the United States), routines through the lens of certain times of day at home and work, or daydreaming through the lens of famous daydreamers.

The Alchemy of Mixing Ideas and Materials

To tackle our three fields we had to develop unconventional ethnographic techniques based on a kind of "analytical alchemy." This means that we experimented with mixes of ideas and materials, for example using a combination of facts and fiction that at first glance do not seem to have anything in common. Although we never got round to questioning teaspoons we followed Georges Perec's advice and looked for both the obvious – things right in front of us, so familiar that they had become invisible – and the overlooked, stuff that might be hiding in all kinds of nooks and crannies.

Besides the usual search for empirical data, we found ourselves working as bricoleurs with at least eight such categories of more or less expected materials, including

memories and autoethnography
interviews and informal surveys
spontaneous and focused observations
ethnographic snapshots
artistic interpretations (from novels to art projects)

media (from newspaper clippings to TV programs)
Google searches of the Internet
readings of cultural history

Observations, Surveys, and Interviews

In the first stage of research, autoethnography turned out to be crucial. How did we ourselves handle waiting, create routines, and daydream, and how did that reflect our own backgrounds as aging white (Swedish) male academics? What kinds of cultural products were we? We started by comparing our memories of Christmas celebrations, work routines, and morning habits, as well as the times and places we tended to choose for our daydreaming. Sometimes we felt that an entire book could be based upon memories and self-observations, and we were reminded how tempting it is to generalize from one's own experiences. Autoethnography is a creative tool that always risks turning into autobiographical writing.

Later we discussed our personal reflections with others and interviewed people in different situations. Looking for contrasts, we conducted informal surveys among students, using a snapshot approach. We asked them questions relating to our three themes, to which they wrote anonymous answers on slips of papers. What do you do when waiting? Tell us about your morning routines. In what situations do you daydream? We hoped to get food for thought, not to make a statistical survey, and in this book we have included only a few of the couple of thousand handwritten answers we collected. Most of the answers are concrete and surprisingly immediate accounts, some laconic, others like short stories on one page.

The answers were anonymous, but we wanted to know whether the writer was male or female, and sometimes the texts also revealed something about class, ethnic background, age, and other personal matters. Thus we collected a great many fragments of the private lives of men and women between the ages of twenty and forty; the group did not, of course, represent a cross-section of Swedish society. We think that the anonymity and the rather unstructured form of narration made it easier for the students to disclose thoughts and behaviors that might otherwise have seemed ridiculous or too private.

Another way of collecting information for this book was that of both spontaneous and focused observations. However, we found ourselves constantly needing to problematize what observations mean and how they are organized. We therefore had to reflect upon how to do ethnographic observations and what happens when they are transformed into descriptions. For example, when one of us tried to make a comparative study of bus queues in Swedish cities and London, it turned out to be difficult to stand and watch people queuing. Nothing seemed to happen. What should one look at – the motionless bodies, or the indifferent faces? It was not until someone tried to jump the queue that it became interesting and worth writing down in the notebook. It was even harder to observe people daydreaming or performing routines. How can one observe invisible or private activities?

But we did not give up, because we discovered that it was not in the moment of observation, when nothing seems to be happening, that we "saw" what was going on. It was when we were verbalizing our impressions – using concepts and metaphors, and describing movements, connections, and processes – that the observations got meaning for us. Above all, it was in writing about them that we were able to transform inconspicuous activities into culturally comprehensible patterns.

Ethnographic Snapshots

While working on this project we became constant collectors, seeing possible material everywhere. Certain situations, texts, and images opened our eyes and redirected our analytical gaze. The invisible adventure at the supermarket with which we opened this book was one such eye-opening observation, as were the wait at the car repair shop and the morning routine putting on makeup. These eye-opening observations did not result entirely by chance; they were to some extent the result of analytical vigilance, for we were more or less unconsciously looking for ideas and materials as we pursued our everyday life. Observations that caught our eye might include an advertisement glimpsed on a bus, an incident at a store, a book on a table, a scene in a movie, a remark by a colleague. Ideas rarely occurred to us while at our desk or watching our computer screen but rather when our bodies were on the move and our minds drifting. The pocket notebook or slip of paper became the organizing medium of such finds.

One category of snapshots came from the stream of media stuff in everyday life. We found ourselves functioning like ethnographic flycatchers while reading newspapers, listening to the radio, and watching television. At any moment we were prepared to see or hear something related to what we were writing about. It might strengthen our ideas or guide them into new directions.

Surfing the Internet was one of the ways we worked through media materials. Googling, reading blogs, and tracking key words helped us to maneuver in the information jungle. Here new forms of serendipity and chance emerged, and this called for reflection.[2] However, we had to know something about what we were looking for and how we should analytically handle material that was publicly communicated for so many different reasons.[3]

Art as Analysis

A special category of media material on which we drew were artistic projects that writers and filmmakers have created on the theme of doing nothing. Among these projects we discovered inspiring experimentation with things that are difficult to put into words or distinct forms – such things as hunches, dream fragments, worn habits. This category includes James Joyce's experiments with turning streams of consciousness into prose, as well as the film about Harold Crick and brushing one's teeth.

In our study we have tried to combine the artist's creative freedom with what Neil Cummings (1993) has called the alienating technique of homeopathic tactics, that is, viewing a certain phenomenon in extreme concentration or dilution. Artists experiment by viewing phenomena from very far away or extremely close up, and by alternating the glance with the concentrated stare.

After having spent so much time with texts on waiting and with trying to observe waiting rooms we found it liberating to watch Akram Khan's ballet Bahok, where eight dancers wait desperately in an airport. The choreographer had dispensed with all distractions: the work consisted entirely of bodies moving in a nondescript gray space. All the microroutines of waiting were exaggerated and dramatized; bodies and bodywork dominated the scene. Suddenly new dimensions emerged.

Harry Lee uses a similar homeopathic technique in her installation The Generic Waiting Room. This work, too, features concentration on a few crucial ingredients, while everything else is stripped away. Standing inside the installation, watching and sensing the bodies moving on the scene, we were able to add yet another dimension of waiting to our analysis.

Searching for Contrasts in Time and Space

The snapshot approach yielded a wealth of material, gleaned from all corners of society; the drawback was, of course, that much of the material lacked context. Therefore we used a historical and contrasting perspective to contextualize the various ways of doing nothing. Whenever we felt caught in our analysis, lacking distance, we found it helpful to use this tool to back away from the present and get a longer view.

Similarly, when we found ourselves stuck in the seeming passivity of waiting, we found it liberating to read about nineteenth-century construction of railway stations and their new waiting rooms. Watching a TV program on the childhood of the Brontë sisters brought back vague memories of their fantasyland project and provided us with a starring point for considering the era of the Romantic early nineteenth century, when daydreaming was a constant topic of discussion.

Historical examples thus sometimes served as revelations. Going back to a time when queuing was a novelty opened up a richer understanding of the phenomenon. What was a queue, what should it look like? How should people be trained to queue?

By looking at the discussion of scientific management in the early twentieth century, when engineers and consultants dreamt about producing "the perfect work routine," we learned that the history of routines includes aspects we had not anticipated. We found similar contrasts when we studied life outside Western mainstream life, as Kapuśiński, for example, showed in his reflections on waiting in Africa, or as we discovered in Swedish rural rituals of keeping dusk.

Navigating the Seas of Earlier Research

We spent much time researching the scholarly literature on our three topics. This was not easy, given that we were dealing with topics that cut across established categories. In some ways it felt as if we were trying to clear paths in a jungle of information, knowing that we would not be able to find everything that could be of use.

Our searches often created chains of references, and often they started with no more than a tip from a colleague, a Googled paper, or a passing reference in a book. Through such references we sometimes ended up in surprising places and above all in unexpected disciplines. We realized that there is a loosely integrated community of scholars who represent a variety of perspectives on doing nothing. Philosophers, geographers, and medical researchers are interested in waiting; psychologists and architects study routines; and historians, sexologists, and even computer researchers discuss dreams. Although they seldom shared our ethnographic take on the topics, they brought interesting new points to light.

We had at our disposal a number of techniques for trawling for information, but it was never possible to do a full sweep – which, moreover, would have drowned the project in material. We used a variety of different search engines. While one of us spent hours Googling the Internet and experiencing the boredom of finding that over 90 percent of the hits are usually useless, the other spent time browsing bookshelves in libraries, bookstores, and second-hand stores. We also often tapped into our personal networks of scholars: "I have heard of a guy you might ask, who remembers reading something..."

Cultural Analysis of Disparate Materials and Practices

The categories of materials we used, listed above, also reveal something about the different modes of searching and mixing we employed. Doing ethnography and cultural analysis of non-events involved a sequence of practices that combined mind work with physical activity. Working our way through a library section, pulling out books and leafing through pages, was a different kind of hunting and gathering than surfing the Internet or standing in the middle of an art installation. Different senses were sparked and set the mind wandering in diverse ways. There is a fundamental difference between staring at people who look like they're waiting and glancing at someone who seems to be performing a routine. Touching a daydreaming prop is not like driving a car through a favorite fantasizing landscape. Sensing the nervousness in the air of a waiting room is quite another thing than listening to a room's telling silence.

Our miscellaneous materials influenced our analytical process and understanding. We are not at all sure where some of the specific ideas and interpretations in this book actually came from. Many of them – for example, the ideas of waiting as "stationary mobility," daydreaming as "mental absence," or routines as "emotional minefields" – seem to have been the result of hunches and sudden associations.

In reconstructing the research process we realized, first, that we had made cultural analysis out of texts, impressions, and practices that were not obviously scientific material. This required our circling the evidence and trying different analytical entrances, metaphors, and concepts.

Second, to make our investigation a cultural analysis we had had to stress certain aspects of individual cases. How were they permeated by norms, rules, and values? Merely by asking in what ways queuing or morning routines are learned, communicated, and symbolically organized made us see these activities in new ways. By treating daydreaming in relation to external factors and as something people practice in social contexts we were able to replace the psychological perspective with a cultural one.

Third, rather than working with "empirical evidence" we searched for "good quotations" and examples that had the potential to open up new understanding. Some of the quotations we found energized us. Fernando Pessoa's bookkeeper, Bernardo, certainly told us things about daydreaming that suited what we had already thought and written, but he also expressed feelings and reflections that we had not anticipated. Ha Jin's novel Waiting forced us to think about what happens when an entire lifetime is organized around a cultural theme.

The quotations sometimes said more than we had expected, and they spilled over with information that forced us to think harder about their meaning. As a result of this kind of second-hand research we constantly switched between the familiar world of already formulated ideas and a strange, incomprehensible world where vague ideas seemed to be waiting for verbal representation.

Fourth, by using theoretical concepts and perspectives we tried to squeeze new understandings out of familiar examples. What did Sartre have to say about bus queues, Roland Barthes about waiting, Mary Douglas about home routines, and Ernst Bloch about daydreams? Thinkers such as these helped us to make the familiar strange.

Finally, we reflected on our project as teamwork. Our aim was to combine our separate thoughts and writings in a unified, seamless text but also to challenge each other's favorite ideas. Given the distance separating us (1,200 kilometers between Lund in the south of Sweden and Umeå in the north), most of our discussions were carried out on the telephone and in e-mail messages. We continually sent revised versions of text to each other, and every time we received them back they were radically changed and developed. Occasionally we had heated discussions whether the change was an improvement or not.

Yet we were surprised by the fact that older technologies of communication are superior to the newer ones. When we met face to face we realized that a one-hour walk discussing the project could provide far more energy and input than a constant stream of electronic attachments. As any fieldworker knows, the "walk and talk" method opens up a wealth of new insights.

We have quite different personalities and research temperaments – one of us more historically oriented, the other more interested in fieldwork, one a bohemian, the other a pedant – so there was never a risk that our cooperation might become too smooth an intellectual confluence. We experienced a good deal of friction while rewriting and deleting, but also a creative blurring of authorship. Even if we can still recognize who was the originator of any one theme, material, or idea, the finished book is a true joint venture in every sentence.

Notes

1   Editorial note: The following essay has originally been published as an appendix to the ethnography "The Secret World of Doing Nothing" (2010), an ethnographic account of what happens if nothing is happening. It has been widely perceived in urban anthropology for its methodology. Hence, it is published here as a 'lent epilogue'.

2   As well as keeping ethical considerations in mind when using the Internet for research purposes, see also the recommendations issued in 2002 by the Association of Internet Researchers, www.aoir.org/reports/ethics.pdf.

3   We found good material at the site http://standinaqueue.wordpress.com, which contains many stories and photographs of people queuing in different places all over the world. No doubt these stories were contributed for the purpose of sharing a boring or frustrating experience and airing opinions about having had to wait. But the stories gave us new insights about how a daily routine such as queuing may express cultural differences and arouse strong emotions, which people evidently felt they needed to communicate and share with strangers.

References

Reading Things, edited by Neil Cummings. London: Chance Books, 1993.

Out in the Field – Comics for an Urban Anthropology

In early 2015 Anja Schwanhäußer approached me with her work on an Urban Anthropology Anthology focusing on methods of participant observation and 'hanging around'. I was immediately interested when she invited me to contribute accompanying illustrations. We started an ongoing discussion on how the academic work of city researchers could be transformed into drawings that add an independent artistic view to the content. We did not want decorative vignettes separating chapters. Comics, very short graphic novels, we agreed, could be an appropriate medium since they allow text and time to be added to the drawings. Comics would make it possible to include dialogues and anecdotes of the actual fieldwork, which forms the basis of most contributions in the book. We chose six essays dealing with different sites and cities. Thus the novels would show a broader diversity of 'fields'.

As I started working on the storytelling, I realized that the content of each single text was complex and multi-layered enough for a comic of its own. Altogether, the amount of information was really growing out of hand. We had to tie things together, find and agree on a focus that unites all six essays. The layout did not allow more than three pages each, so the story had to be short and to the point.

Eventually, the notion that the researcher's personality cannot be left out in the peering process of fieldwork became the conjunctive element in all the works. The 'Researcher's Fear of the Field' as Rolf Lindner once coined it. Why not bring this aspect to the center of the comic and to the attention of the reader?

Historically as well as in mood and atmosphere, the emergence of the Chicago School of Sociology is connected to the hardboiled era and film noir. Film noir is associated with low-key black-and-white visuals, derived from German Expressionist cinematography of the 1920s and 1930s. Much of the attitude of classic noir is rooted in the hardboiled school of crime fiction that emerged in the United States during the Great Depression. It generated a stock character, hard as bone, a lonely wolf out in the big cities' rough streets. This became the aesthetic foundation for the short novels. Once this formal decision was made, I sent sketches of first storyboards to the authors. Instead of explaining the project verbally, I presented the drawings as an invitation for a dialogue.

Sending a storyboard out to someone I had never met or talked to was quite a challenge, since my comics tell a moment of the person's life as I imagine it. Certainly I would deliver an artistic interpretation that presumably will be very different from what really happened. Yet knowing the protagonist of my comic will also be its reader, a reader who would know the original situation better than I, the author, did make me anxious. All six academics agreed immediately when I confronted them with the idea of creating a comic about their personal tenseness in the fieldwork.

The first storyboard I sent to Les Back was about him meeting his brother Ken in a football stadium in south London. The comic was a reference to his text 'Inscriptions of Love' and touched the issue of writing about a sensitive family topic, tattoos in this case.

Les did not agree on the setting I chose for the comic as he never went to Millwall stadium with Ken. 'So', he wrote 'I think the context seems not quite right. Also, the dialogue between us jars a little – it isn't how we would talk to each other but I could help you with that if you'd like me to. I could re-write the dialogue so that it would feel more like the way we would talk.' We agreed the novel should take place at a trailer park in Norman's Bay, where they often used to go with the entire family. Les sent me a couple of family photos and a scripted dialogue two days later. Photographs, the analytic essay 'Inscriptions of Love', and the text Les wrote are fragments that have actually been said and documented. Additionally Les included personal inner conflicts in the siblings' relationship as part of the dialogue. As a result the comic got very intimate. The brotherly differences are details connected to Les as a researching personality and an aspect I would not get to know by reading his book or interviews. Combining, interpreting, and redrawing the elements, adding the windy atmosphere of the British coast to the emotional conversation of two brothers led to a result that can be called 'true fiction', as Les has put it.

The medium of comic allows to leave space for the unspoken. Being able to print this silence in a book offers space for the reader to interpret the interpreted.

The 'Researcher's Fear of the Field' is interesting substance for novelists. It shows two worlds touching that seem to be quite far apart sometimes: academia and 'real' life. Peeling out the researcher's relation to the object of interest brought a subliminal and very personal net of correlation to the center of the short graphic novels. Collaborating with 'real' protagonists and drawing their stories made it clear to me how easily the fine line between truth and fiction blurs and that academia is also part of this 'real' life, after all.

In October 2015, Nele Brönner

Acknowledgements

I would like to thank Peter Neitzke (†) for initiating this project. Thanks also to Stefan Klinker, Martin Mittelmeier, Jan-Frederik Bandel, Angela Dressler, Sebastian de Morelos, Patrik Schwarz and Nicola Behrmann for inspiring conversations. Most of all, thank you to all the authors I contacted who kindly gave their permission to reprint their writing.

References

Howard S. Becker. "Learning to observe in Chicago." From the author's website, www. howardsbecker. com. A French version has been published in *Le goût de l'observation,* by Jean Peneff, Paris: La Découverte, 2009.

Peter Jackson. "Urban Ethnography." From *Progress in Human Geography* 1985: 9, 157.

Les Back. "Inscriptions of Love." From *The Art of Listening.* Oxford et al.: Berg, 2007.

Ruth Behar. "My Mexican Friend Marta Who Lives Across the Border from Me in Detroit." From *The Vulnerable Observer. Anthropology That Breaks Your Heart,* by Ruth Behar. Boston: Beacon Press, 1996.

Moritz Ege. "Carrot-cut Jeans: An Ethnographic Account of Assertiveness, Embarrassment and Ambiguity in the Figuration of Working-class Male Youth Identities in Berlin." From *Global Denim,* edited by Daniel Miller and Sophie Woodward. Oxford et.al.: Berg, 2011.

Rolf Lindner. "The Imaginary of the City." From *The Contemporary Study of Culture,* edited by Bundesministerium für Wissenschaft und Verkehr and Internationales Forschungszentrum Kulturwissenschaften. Wien: Turia + Kant, 1999.

Orvar Löfgren and Billy Ehn. "Appendix: Doing an Ethnography of "Non-events"." From *The Secret World of Doing nothing* by Orvar Löfgren and Billy Ehn. © 2010 by the Regents of the University of California. Published by the University of California Press.

Jonathan Raban. "The City as Melodrama." From *Soft City* by Jonathan Raban. London: Picador, 2008. Copyright © Jonathan Raban 2008.

Mirko Zardini. "Toward a sensorial urbanism." Introductory essay from: *Sense of the City. An Alternate Approach to Urbanism,* edited by Mirko Zardini. Montreal: Canadian Centre of Architecture; Zürich: Lars Müller Publishers, 2005.

Margarethe Kusenbach. "The go-along method." Extracted from "Street phenomenology. The go-along as ethnographic research tool". From *Ethnography* vol. 4, 3, 2003.

Loïc Wacquant. "Urban Desolation and Symbolic Denigration in the Hyperghetto." Expanded version from *Social Psychology Quarterly* 20, no. 3 (September 2010): 1–5, also published in: *Dérive. Zeitschrift für Stadtforschung* Oct–Dec 2010, 40/41.

Authors

Les Back Professor of Sociology at Goldsmiths, University of London. His anthropology of popular culture explores racism and social inequality. In his ethnographic research, which is often based in south London, he expands the boundaries of academic methodology towards literature, photography and new media. His book *The Art of Listening* (2007) promotes listening as a metaphor for aesthetic sensibility. Formerly working at the Department of Cultural Studies, University of Birmingham, he is among those who introduced cultural studies to anthropology. He has initiated and led several highly paid research projects. Books (selected titles): *The Art of listening* (2007). *Live methods* (2013). Website: www.academic-diary.co.uk. He also writes journalism.

Howard S. Becker Sociologist and jazz-piano-player, who made major contributions to the sociology of deviance, sociology of art, and sociology of music. His classic study *Outsiders* (1963) was one of the first to introduce labelling theory, arguing that deviance is not a quality of a bad person, but the result of someone defining someone's activity as bad. He has received honorary doctorates in universities in France, Germany and Great Britain. Books (selected titles): *Outsiders. Studies in the Sociology of Deviance* (1963). *Art Worlds* (1982). *Telling About Society* (2007). Website: www.howardsbecker.com. Born in 1928 in Chicago, he is a leading figure in Chicago School Sociology and its most popular contemporary protagonist.

Ruth Behar Cuban-American anthropologist, filmmaker, writer, poet and a leading figure in feminist anthropology. She advocates storytelling in anthropology and the acknowledgement of the subjective nature of research. She reached world fame for her book *Translated Woman* (1993), about the encounter between her and a Mexican street peddler and the mutual desires that bind together anthropologists and their subjects. She works as Professor of Anthropology at the University of Michigan. Books (selected titles): *Translated Woman* (1993). *The Vulnerable Observer* (1996). Website: www.ruthbehar.com. In 1999, Latina Magazine named her one of 50 Latinas who made history in the twentieth century.

Nele Brönner Berlin-based visual artist, author and illustrator. Her artistic work blurs the line between research, art and academia. Current artistic research deals with transformations of cities like Berlin, Lagos and Cairo. In 2015, her children's book *Affenfalle* won the Serafinapreis of the Deutsche Akademie für Kinder- und Jugendliteratur. Her work is published in various journals such as *ZEIT online, taz, Le Monde diplomatique, FAZ, Stadtaspekte.*

Moritz Ege   Professor for Cultural Anthropology and European Ethnology at the Georg-August-University Göttingen. His work on the figure of the "Proll" (chav) has been a cornerstone in the ethnographic study of social inequality in Germany. He argues that popular culture, fashion and style play a crucial role in structuring society. Books (selected titles): *„Ein Proll mit Klasse." Mode, Popkultur und soziale Ungleichheiten unter jungen Männern in Berlin (2013). Schwarzwerden. „Afroamerika-nophilie" in den 1960er und 1970er Jahren (2007).* He currently leads the project *Moskau – Urbane Ethik des Protests und Gewalt der Ethik.*

Billy Ehn   Ethnologist and Professor Emeritus at the University of Umeå, Sweden. He published various ethnographic studies. As a field researcher, he has lived in Poland and in former Yugoslavia, he worked in a factory and a nursery. Books (selected titles): *Exploring everyday life. Strategies for Ethnography and Cultural Analysis* (2015, with Orvar Löfgren and Richard Wilk). *The Secret World of Doing Nothing* (2010, with Orvar Löfgren).

Peter Jackson   Professor of Human Geography at the University of Sheffield. He wrote his classic essay "Urban Ethnography" during his American Studies Fellowship at the University of Chicago, defining urban ethnography as the study of contemporary society. His current research focuses on social and cultural geography, consumption and identity, families and food. Books (selected titles): *Anxious Appetites: Food and Consumer Culture* (2015). *Food Words (2013)* and the *Handbook of Food Research (2013).* Besides his academic work, he also chairs the Food Standards Agency's Social Science Research Committee. Website: Food Stories.

Margarethe Kusenbach   Associate Professor of Sociology at the University of South Florida. Her essay about the go-along method has been widely perceived within the field of urban research. She explores the ways in which people adapt to unfamiliar social and physical environments, and how they come to belong, or not, within new places and communities. Books (selected titles): *Home: International*

Perspectives on Culture, Identity, and Belonging (2013, with Krista Paulsen). For her forthcoming book she conducts research about issues of identity and community among people living in mobile homes and mobile home communities within the Tampa Bay region.

Rolf Lindner   Sociologist, Cultural Analyst and Professor Emeritus at the Department of European Ethnology at the Humboldt-University Berlin. He advocates sociological imagination and the diversity of fieldwork data. Being among the ones who introduced Urban Anthropology and Cultural Studies to Germany, he wrote introductory books, where he executed the methods of these fields on themselves. In his classic study on the Chicago School Sociology, he unravelled the roots of 20th century urban sociology in journalism. In the 1970s, he was one of the first sociologists studying punk subculture. Recently, he was among the founders of the degree program *Culture of the Metropoles* at the Hafen-City-University Hamburg. Books (selected titles): *The reportage of urban culture. Robert Park and the Chicago School* (1996). *Die Stunde der Cultural Studies* (2000). His essay „Die Angst des Forschers vor dem Feld" (1981, The researcher's fear of the field), which promotes the problems and obstacles of the field as important data, is the baseline for Nele Brönner's comics in this book.

Orvar Löfgren   Professor Emeritus of Ethnology at the University of Lund and a leading figure in European Ethnology. His cultural analysis embraces close readings of everyday life culture and questions on how to study it. Books (selected titles): *Exploring everyday life. Strategies for Ethnography and Cultural Analysis* (2015, with Billy Ehn). *The Secret World of Doing Nothing* (2010, with Billy Ehn).

Jonathan Raban   British travel writer, novelist and former professor of literature. He has received several important book awards, including the Royal Society of Literature's Heinemann award. The close and sensible observation of urban and contemporary culture is a continuous thread through his work. Books (selected titles): *Soft City* (1974). *Driving home: An American Journey* (2011). He lives quite a secluded life style in Seattle.

Anja Schwanhäußer Berlin-based freelance urban anthropologist and street artist. She teaches urban anthropology at Humboldt-University Berlin and published several books on this topic with a focus on subculture and field research. Earlier projects include the international research project "Culture of Cities. Toronto, Montreal, Berlin, Dublin" (York University, Toronto), where she owned a fellowship. Books (selected titles): *Kosmonauten des Underground. Ethnografie einer Berliner Szene (2010). Orte. Situationen. Atmosphären – Kulturanalytische Skizzen* (2010, with Beate Binder, Moritz Ege, Jens Wietschorke). She currently works as project researcher at the Academy of Science in Vienna.

Loïc Wacquant Professor of Sociology at the University of California, Berkeley, and Researcher at the Centre de sociologie européenne, Paris. He is a sharp critic of social inequality in the neoliberal age and among the leading ethnographers in his field. In his ethnography *Body and Soul* (2004), he reports about a boxing gym in a Chicago ghetto, choosing an approach he calls "carnal sociology" in order to grasp the sensual aspects of culture. He has published many books and essays that were perceived within academia and beyond, which made him a public intellectual. His book "Invitation to Reflexive Sociology" (1992, with Pierre Bourdieu) has been translated in 19 languages. Books (selected titles): *Body and Soul: Ethnographic Notebooks of An Apprentice-Boxer* (2004). *Das Janusgesicht des Ghettos und andere Essays* (2006). *Urban Outcasts: A Comparative Sociology of Advanced Marginality* (2008). He is co-founder and editor of the interdisciplinary journal *Ethnography*.

Mirko Zardini Director of the Canadian Centre for Architecture (CCA) in Montreal, Canada, curator of prize-winning exhibitions. He is not only a practicing architect, but a researcher into the urban landscape whose publications expand the realm of architecture toward contemporary culture and city life. Books (selected titles): *Sense of the City. An Alternate Approach to Urbanism* (2006). *Rooms You May Have Missed* (2014). Exhibitions: *Actions: What You Can Do With The City* (2008). *1973: Sorry, out of Gas* (2007–08). Since 2005, as director, Zardini has overseen the transformation of the CCA to address contemporary social, political and environmental issues.

**Harald Bodenschatz, Piero Sassi,
Max Welch Guerra (eds.)**

Urbanism and Dictatorship

A European Perspective

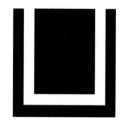

Urban design under European dictatorships in the first
half of the twentieth century must be considered in an international context, as the professional and cultural exchange
between European countries was – beyond conflicts and
political orientations – very intensive. This European perspective is likewise an expression of our culture of memory:
our ability to recognize old and new forms of dictatorship!

248 pages, 100 b/w-illustrations, softcover
(BWF 153) ISBN: 978-3-03821-660-5
Urbanism

**Mary Dellenbaugh, Markus Kip,
Majken Bieniok, Agnes Katharina Müller,
Martin Schwegmann (eds.)**

**Urban Commons:
Moving Beyond State and Market**

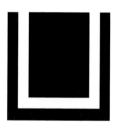

In recent years, the concept of commons has gained popularity, as it promises a more participatory form of gover-
nance than state tutelage, and more equity in addressing
human needs than the market. This publication explores
the struggle for urban commons through a variety of case
studies from Berlin to Hyderabad, Santiago and Seoul and
asks what is specifically "urban" about them.

244 pages, 21 b/w-illustrations, softcover
(BWF 153) ISBN: 978-3-03821-661-2
Urbanism

Bauwelt Fundamente (selected titles)

All titles are available as well as e-book.   More Bauwelt Fundamente on: degruyter.com